Learn photography a different way

by

Davor Pavlic

2019

Table of Contents

11

13

17

Introduction

The idea for this collection of quotes of various authors was born combining two things I always actually liked. For one... I always loved the old latin sentences from various philosophers etc. I've known some of those way before I actualy had latin class for the first time. And the second thing is... Love for photography and the wish to always learn more and advance as a photographer.

Photography came across my path some time when I was a lot younger and film cameras were still holding their ground pretty nicely. Even though I didn't own a film SLR I was even then learning some basics, to make every shot count and so on. Some time later I got a digital compact camera and we were pretty much inseparable. I was always shooting and always learning step-by-step. In 2009 I am buying my first dSLR which was very soon replaced by a more advanced version. In the same year I was joining the local photoclub „Tuzla".

In all this time I am spending time watching pictures in the windows of photography studios as a kid, especialy when one of my very early photographs from my compact film camera was exibited in one studio, to reading books and magazines, visiting sites, watching YouTube videos, posting photos on various portals to get critique.

And in all this process every book or site or clip that I came across was either saying something about the technical aspects of photography and how to get a shot, what smaler aperture does and so on or visualy by showing pictures how something should look like. So now, instead of that I wanted to make a collection resembling latin sentences from which photographers can learn as much as from any book dealing with techical aspects of photography, only in a different way and maybe on a different level. One might know how to set ISO, aperture, exposure, white balance, etc., but there is also much power in a simple sentence „If your pictures aren't good enough, you're not close enough" by Robert Capa which says so much more than a simple instruction that you need to fill the frame or the best sentence for begginers who think their photography will improve with gear „The best camera is the one that's with you" by Chase Jarvis.

This goes also all the way to understanding the philosophy of some authors and can lead to understanding them better and their works, but it is also a collection of directions on how to improve yourself, your approach and your photography.

Apart from all the usefull and serious quotes there are also some funny ones, because in the end, photography isn't easy to do as many might think and even if it's not a profession it's a very expensive hobby and art and it's nice to have something to come back to or think of something that will make you smile a bit when you buy that new lens you so much wanted or some other piece of equipment that wasn't cheap at all.

Many of these quotes you can find all over the internet, some have even very nice databases of them, but I wanted to step this up a notch and taken some quotes out of books, training videos, YouTube clips and personal contact with some of the world known photographers in which they have given some of their opinions on photography you can not find anywhere else. In this collection there are over 400 authors.

But even so, I do not want to start and end only with quotations, so I'll also have a little bit about photography and some articles I have written for a website I used to have. One of them also being an article on how to charge for photography and a formula behind it.

Photography

We can't really create a book about photography without doing at least some introduction, but I'll try to be as brief as possible.

The known film photography started in 1925. A century after it started as camera obscura – a technique that was liked by some painters. This was a dark room in which a ray of light was released and that ray would be projecting the picture on a background the painter was painting on – painting with light or photo-graphy. And to consider that painters used to be against photography being called an art... Leica, which was then released as a camera that shoots on 32 mm film was shooting on 2:3 ratio, which is a standard dimension even today. And the first modern film in color was released in 1935.

Why are we talking about this type of photography? Because even todays cameras, even the digital ones, are built on this principle – a mobile camera obscura. The lens which controls how much light comes through the aperture, what is behind the lens is the dark room and even further back is the medium on which it is recording – film or a digital sensor.

The digital photography started when Sony first found a CCD sensor instead of the film. The camera that marked that change was Sony Mavica. Mavica can't really be called a fully digital camera, because even though it was recording on a disk, the photographs were only viewed on the television.

In 1990 Kodak goes a step further and presents to the public the first comercially available digital camera, which, because of the price, was available only to reporters and for professional use.

When transitioning from analogue to digital photography the thoughts of professional photographers were divided around transitioning or not. And the ones who didn't transition to digital were actually right. It was a new technology which wasn't still perfected and it had some downsides, one of which is the lower photograph quality. But with the development of cameras professional photographers were slowly transitioning to digital, pleased with the posibilities the technology provides after some of the details were fixed.

Besides the manipulation possibilites of digital photographs, photographers transitioned to digital also because of the price. Although the digital cameras may have been expensive, in the long run it was cheaper and easier for people who were shooting multiple rolls of film and didn't need to carry boxes of those or write which photo was which, etc. It is also cheaper because that every shot doesn't cost you money now. Instead it's only ones and zeroes and you didn't need to travel to a studio to see if the photograph was a success or not.

If we were to compare analogue and digital cameras we would inadvertently come to pixels. So, if that is what you are into, here's a few comparissons. Even though film doesn't have pixels, but lines, translated to pixels, it would probably be around 20 MP. At the time of preparing the book for the first time, this was more than a regular compact camera, now even the telephones have more. Even the higher end professional cameras for a long time had only 12 MP or even less. The 20 MP film shot is considered a photograph taken under good conditions. When those conditions change it is possible for the MP value to go down as far as 4 MP.

But let's not get hung up on pixels. Megapixel number was for a very long time just a marketing trick which meant nothing. While Canon was bumping up Megapixels, Nikon was maxed for a long time at 13 MP cameras. Because of this at that time Nikon had a higher performance in lower light conditions. Besides, to this day I sometimes exhibit a photograph that I had done with a 5 MP camera – Canon Powershot A95.

And while some were leading discussions about photography being art or not and possibly even the megapixel war that got lost along the way, today these discussions boil down to if something went through Photoshop or not.

But the masses aren't really fault for thinking like that. It's the number of the cameras, even the professional ones. Not to menton the telephones, not being able to pick up one and not find 2 or 3 camera lenses on it. The photographs made on a phone and a compact camera aren't really that bad. But most of the improvements in that field for a long time were only MP increases. Now, there has been some improvements in this area, especially with 2 and 3 main camera lenses, but it still doesn't compare to a dSLR, no matter how many comercials phone companies make using those very images. They especially lose quality in low light conditions.

The arrival of digital cameras, cameras getting cheaper and more accessible, changing the film with memory cards so that every shutter click isn't costing you money... Add internet to this and you get the formula for everyone thinking they are the next Ansel Adams.

If, or, rather, when we get to a good photograph we will most likely find a comment somewhere that there is too much photoshop. Hell, even some photography portals are doing this, so why would someone else be held to a higher standard? But people need to understand that there was a Photoshop even before the Photoshop. People have always been touching up photographs, even layering was available, the only problem was that you needed to have a lot of skill, a lot of time and a lot of patience.

So, even though I am not the biggest fan of the tool called Photoshop, that is all that it is – a tool. It's the dark room of today. When we are shooting RAW photographs to save a better quality digital negative, we need to do at least some basic manipulations. Or would everyone like us to beliewe that #IwokeUpThisWay and that Instagram doesn't have filters and that selfie cameras don't have softening built into them?

I hope that we can reconcile that photography has evolved again and just like it changed from camera obscura to film, it can change again. We cannot hold it to standard from 100 years ago and much more important than what tools we use is our vision, our artistic view and interpretation and our continuing education in our fields.

This is why I imagined this book to be a different kind of book about photography, because there are others that will teach you about the rule of thirds and composition, but you can also learn some other things about it in a different way. You could learn how to charge for your photography and you can get to many conclustions just by reading quotes about photography and art.

How to charge for your photography

If you are an emerging photographer and you are just starting to charge for your photography there are a couple of how to's. The good thing is, you are thinking about it and you should be paid because you are providing service as anyone else.

Breaking it down

If photography is your hobby-turned-job, which would say your second job or your family member is supporting it by having a job too and you're home based without a studio – well, you already have it much easier.

In the beginning you will probably be working for free while building a portfolio, doing charity or meeting people you know have connections and can recommend you. Those are the only situations you can work for free on occasion. And always be holding on to one thought: *„ Work for free or for full price, but never for cheap"* by Paul Scriven.

To straighten out a few things… You need to define your success. How many weddings a year (if you are a wedding photographer, if not, then insert your field) would you be satisfied with? Always have „or more". 10 or more. 20 or more. 50 or more.

How to charge for your photography formula

First of all, when it comes to how to charge for your photography formula you have to know that there are no magic numbers and nobody can tell you to charge a certain amount for your work. Even though we run from math and formulas, there is actually a formula to how to charge for your photography and it is quite simple. OK, there isn't really, this is my formula of pricing your photography. The formula is this:

- How well-known photographer are you – recognition/reputation – R.
- Based on your reputation level you will also be deciding how much you charge for the clients you had to decline to work with. At level 1 it will be 0 because you are able to get to all the clients, at level 2 it's 5% and at level 5 it's 20% maximum. Multiply with, as goes, 1; 1.05; 1.10; 1.15; 1.20. Don't go over the top with it. Declined clients – d.
- Your pay – Y – Y=w*t
- How long does it take – time – t
- Determine how much you ask for an hour of your time and how much would you ask for a half day and full day. Your initial hourly price will follow you to level 3, then you can adjust it on level 4 and 5. How much is your time worth – worth – w
- Even if the cameras aren't getting any smaller the more we shoot, they are consumables. The manufacturers usually say you need to service your shutter once every 200.000 photographs. If you shoot 1.000 photographs that's 0.5%. In my inquiry that is around $300. So you can charge 5% of that every shoot. – Consumables – c
- You also could and should copyright your photographs. There is a website you can register a batch of photographs, no matter is it 10 or 10.000 – the fee is around $30-$35 per one batch. I believe the website is copyright.gov. This is one of the greatest investments, as you will have much less to deal with if your photograps get stolen. – Copyright – C
- How much are your expenses for props for THAT shoot, not the ones you already have. If

you have no expenses for props, then you charge $1. – props – P

- How much are you paying for renting gear. If you have no expenses for renting gear then you charge $1. – renting gear – g
- How much are the costs of getting to the location. If you have no expenses for travel, then you charge $1. – travel to location – s
- How much you are paying for the assistant. If you have no assistant, then you charge $1. – paying the assistant – a – a=Y/2 (if he is a second shooter) or a=Y/3 (if he is only learning and helping you with gear) (you will have to agree on rates, this is only so you can get a feel for the formula)
- Is it for personal use or for something a client is intending to be making money on – usage – u
- Some suggest you multiply your expenses by at least 2 so you can be making some money and not going back to 0. We will be using percentage. Doubling that amount might be just too much and when you reach higher reputation levels you will have a higher multiplier anyway, which gives you more incentive to be better. – multiplier – m (this is how much you profit)
- Define your regular gear. I like to call this a variable constant. Your regular gear can be 1 body, 2 lenses, 2 strobes, battery, memory cards, reflector. Your essentials. Everyone's essentials can be different. For every other group of essentials you will be adding one more. So... Regular gear (r) = 1. If you're carrying lightstands, battery packs add +1. If there are some other things (a group of those) add 1.
- Product you are offering. This is albums, CDs, prints, etc. – product – p

When determining the numbers take in consideration national average pay or hourly rate. Also, more often than not, take in consideration your environment. Sometimes, some places you can charge more than others, somewhere it's less.

Back to the how to charge for you photography formula now... Just for easier calculation let's say your hourly rate is $5 and you're working 8 hours, including the post production.

$$m(P+p+g+s+c+C+r)+d[R(Y+a)]$$

To put the formula to use, let's say you just finished your portfolio building and your rep is only 1.
Your hourly rate is 5 and you're working for 8 hours.
You are paying your assistant half of that.
You had to buy $25 of props.
You had $30 costs of getting to the location, getting food and water.
You want to earn 20% (profit).
You're charging 5% of servicing your camera shutter – $15.
You're paying $30 for registering copyright.
And you rented $300 worth of gear.
And $50 worth of products.

I'm intentionally forgetting the usage. You will be adding a certain percentage to those if the client is intending to make money with your work. Say 25%, more or less, all up to you. You will need to take care when doing this, because even if some paper is doing something on a bigger scale, they may have a budget and if you don't do it for X amount of dollars, someone else will and it may be even worse than what you are doing.

With numbers it looks like this:

$Y=w*t$

$=5*8$

$=40$

$a=Y/2$

$=40/2$

$=20$

$m(P+p+g+s+c+C+r)+d[R(Y+a)]=$

$1.20(25+50+300+30+15+30+1)+1[1(40+20)]=$

$1.20\times406+60=541,2+60=601,2$

If you had more reputation, you would be earning $1094,4 or more, depending on the level of reputation. The reputation is something you can't learn, you will be rising in reputation by working and delivering quality. You could say that reputation/recognition = demand. If demand for your services is high and you need to choose only 1 client you will be charging the client you have taken for the ones you could have while working with him. You're not charging 5 times more if five more people want you, but you charge some compensation.

And then add +25% if the photographs aren't for personal use, but for commercial.

Negotiating

You won't be holding onto this how to charge for your photography formula as set in stone either. There might be some negotiation needed to get the job and the price everyone is satisfied with – the client and you. When doing negotiations always have in mind clients budget you asked prior to it. When a client tells you the budget you usually match it, never go below. But when a client asks you if you can lower your price, you usually accept, but always ask something in return. Usually what you ask is for your name and/or logo to be on the image they will be using. It most likely will not be getting you any new clients and money, but it is one way of giving in to the client by not letting them know that. So when lowering the price always ask for credit.

Fine art

If you're selling your fine art you can partially use the how to charge for your photography formula, but also take in consideration the dimensions of your photograph (which would be falling into the product part of the formula), how many of the same photograph are you selling. If it's only one you price it accordingly. But you don't sell any more of those. If it's more than one, then you price it lower, but you sell it more than once.

Studio

If you own a studio, then that formula could be a little bit wider and that includes looking into all your expenses and taking all of them into consideration, so if you want to you can tweak it to your needs. Mark has a wonderful video about this too, so you can look it up here[1].

Conclusion

That would be my how to charge for your photography formula and most of the calculating part.

If you're feeling uncomfortable charging for your photography even with using the how to charge for your photography formula, please read this[2].

---

[1] https://youtu.be/OZj16RmtFeg
[2]   http://zarias.tumblr.com/post/50036594150/ive-never-felt-comfortable-taking-money-for

Hourly earnings

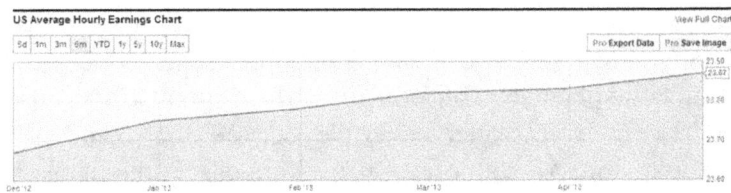

According to the Bureau of Labor Statistics the US average hourly earnings in past six months were only going up. The hourly earnings for April 2013 is $23.87 and, as I said before in how to charge for your photography formula, you will keep this in mind when determining your hourly earnings for your service.

Don't take this too literally... You won't be charging $23.87 an hour, but you want to get to know the economy around you and what people around you can afford. When you do that, you will have a minimum package deal for the majority of average people who can afford you and then add at least two more packages with more value.

Hourly earnings – don't undervalue yourself

Again... You're not charging $23.87 an hour, many people are inventing their hourly earnings, so some are getting $20, some charge $1500 for their services. Don't undervalue yourself. With the current average, for ten hours of work (including post production) you are getting $238.70, excluding all the other stuff you are charging for. So, feel free to value your hourly earnings more. At this point I want to suggest you watch Marks video[3] about charging for photography and there is a nice part about not charging for an hour, but half day and full day values.

---

[3] https://youtu.be/OZj16RmtFeg

Some things that will increase your hourly earnings, because you can't charge sometimes for half day sessions when you're working only 1 hours or close to it, are the customer experience you provide and the amount and quality of services. If you offer exclusive service the price will be exclusive too. If you offer follow-up gifts and thank you cards... well, you're not charging for them or they wouldn't be gifts, but those are the experiences and services, among others, that will raise you above the others. And once you get to a certain point people will stop comparing you only to other photographers, but will start doing so for all the other businesses too. Once you're there, you're the king of the hill.

Photographer level – how to determine your reputation

This is the explanation of the reputation (R) part of the how to charge for your photography formula using the photographer level as a reference.

Intro

As I'm starting to write this and break down the photographer level of reputation I'm finding out it's not easy to do. I'm not sure what I should be taking as the most important criteria for that.

Time? It depends. Some will be better at it and they will need less time to advance their reputation, some will need a little more time. So I can't tell you to advance to next level in a set number of months.

Service? Someone could be giving the best service and some bonuses, but the images would be not as good as someones who is only providing the images and a CD.

Skills? Well, you could be a love child of Joe McNally and Susan Sontag if time travel would be invented, but you still need to get people to recognize them. Or you could be a regular Joe McJolly, learning as you go and still have more skills in getting people to recognize you.

The only logical formula for reputation/recognition would be measuring your demand. If there is a high demand for you then you could say that your reputation is up. If you get an occasional job here and there, then your reputation is low and isn't rising.

But for the needs of this article we'll probably need to use a combination of them all, to set some transitions through photographer levels.

Photographer level

Photographer level 0 (0-999)

This is your level when you are working on your portfolio which you will use to get jobs later. Even if someone suggests they want to pay you something you could accept that, but the question is should you. We go back to that Paul Scriven saying: „Work for free or for full price, never for cheap". So not to get „This guy is cheap" reputation if you are getting any money at this level, then only take compensation for your travel expenses. At this point you are probably not renting gear and investing in many props. That usually comes later.

Even though I said you can also work for free when it's a charity and/or when it's a well connected person/agent who can recommend you to many other people you can charge, this is not a level 0 shooting. You can be the highest level there is and still shoot for free. In these two cases you multiply your end cost with 0.

Also, in both those cases you will present your real value and an invoice. Even if you don't profit, you clearly state your value. At later stages this helps you in two ways.

- You help your client perceive your value even though you are working for free because it's charity or making connections.
- You can probably, can't speak for all countries, do something to lower your tax by presenting your charity work.

At this point you don't have any clients. People you are working with are more in a collaborative relationship with you, than a client-supplier relationship.

Photographer level 1 (1000-1999)

At this point you can even leave out the R from the equation, but you can also leave it, just to get used to it.

This is actually the beginner photographer level. At level 0 you were preparing to be a beginner. This is the level where you are starting to build a reputation and starting at 1. This is the level of photographers who have finished their first portfolio and are just starting out to charge for their photography services. At the early stages I would not suggest using the bonus level.

No matter how good you could have been at level 0, I wouldn't advise skipping levels. As I said, reputation is not something you learn, it's something you earn over time by producing quality work and having satisfied clients. Having a couple of satisfied clients is not the reason to advance to a higher level, especially if you're starting out with family and friends.

Quantity? Let's say you are an event photographer, it doesn't have to be a wedding, and we will say that level one means that you can accept everyone who asks to hire you. This number is 6 clients per month who are asking you for an event. No matter if it's a wedding, a corporate client who needs you for a couple of days or anything similar to it. At this point you add the stay in a hotel to your expenses (include it in travel expense). And, this number of clients does not include the clients who come for a normal ID shot.

Photographer level 2 (2000-2999)

The next best level you can get to. This would mean your reputation is increasing and you are earning more money for your services based on your name. Yes, your name. And it is getting you money, again, because you are getting recognized as someone producing quality work, so do it.

As your reputation advances with each level you have more to lose. So, in order to protect that reputation you will have to be taking more care about your gear and carry more at the same time. This means you carry more memory cards, spare batteries, but most importantly a second body in case the one you are working with breaks for any reason. Now comes gear renting in play. Or getting a second body in any way – buying, asking a friend… You don't need to have two of the same cameras, but it would be nice if the brand is the same at least, so you don't need to be adjusting to it on the job.

Most importantly, you need to quantify your increase in clients. I would suggest you rise in photographer level every time you rise in number of clients or demand for you by 25%, but at the lower levels it would be almost no increase, so we will do it a little bit differently. You can consider yourself a photographer level two when you are at a number of 12 potential clients and need to decline half of those.

If you actually own a studio, then a different approach could also be considered. That approach would be determining how many percent have your sales increased and been there 4-6 months constantly. But that's a bit different approach and a different article.

Don't forget the service you're providing and what you should be aware of while working. It's equally important.

Photographer level 3 (3000-3999)

Numerically, at photographer level three you are having 16 potential clients and have to decline more than half of them.

You are advancing even more. At this point you don't take care only about your gear always working and at the ready very fast so you don't miss any key moments, but have someone else do it for you. This would mean you are hiring an assistant which is helping you with everything. Adjusting lights, changing lenses, helping posing if needed... everything.

At the beginning you might be looking for your assistants, but one indicator of your value rising, even though not necessarily reputation, is when assistants come looking for you. This is applied through the whole photographer level process.

Photographer level 4 (4000-4999)

Now that you are getting more and more proficient at doing what you do the line between the higher levels gets thinner by each level in the quality aspect of your service and it's only some details that you are improving on. It is at this stage that I would suggest using the bonus level for creating a bigger gap between you and other photographers.

In the quantity aspect you will be working with 21 potential clients, so your demand is almost four times higher than your base demand.

You will also be caring about capturing same moments from more angles and more moments all together. So how can you be at two places at the same time? You can't. You hire an assistant which can also be your second shooter. If you find an assistant who will be working exclusively with you in time he can see what your style is, what you are going for and shoot similar photographs. Don't forget to agree with your second shooter who can use those photographs and for what.

Photographer level 5 (5000-5999)

Your reputation is now so high that you are doing everything in your power to keep it at the maximum. Why do you want it at the maximum? Because you want to be better than the other level 5 shooters and you want to be hired, not them. So, if the top score is 5999 points, you are trying to be there. Almost going to level 6, if there would be one. How do you do this?

You are getting at photographer level 5+ by giving nice bonuses to your clients, packaging, CDs, memory sticks, nice bags, greeting cards, thank you cards for hiring you and anything you can come up with that you think will increase your reputation with your client. Because… referrals happen. Divorces too.

The demand for you is exactly 5 times higher than the base demand, so you will be juggling with 30 potential event clients. Next to quality and quantity this level has one more aspect to it and that is that you will need to hire more people if you want to meet your clients wishes and do it all on time.

Bonus photographer level (PS)

Add to your reputation 0,5 points if you are very good at Photoshop. This does not mean you are good at adding contrast, brightening or darkening the image, cropping and some other simple tasks. This means that you are proficient at Photoshop and able to go into each and every pixel if needed and you can offer a work of art to your client if he wants that.

Now, don't get me wrong, photography is a work of art on it's own, but you can offer one piece that will be fine art, a composit if needed. To get to this level you will need images you can make composites from. So some interesting walls, skies, buildings, textures, alley ways, balloons, etc. Some of those you can photograph for the purpose of the client you're working for at that moment, some you will need to be collecting for some time.

If you want to add this to your reputation be prepared to work on your photographs like Ben Willmore says: untill you run out of patience, time or problems. I suggest you don't run out of first two, only the latter.

But don't worry, you're charging for the time you're investing in post production also.

Usage – How it relates to pricing your photography

I would like to address a few more issues with charging for your photography and hopefully clear some things up. In this article I will address when you do not charge more for a certain usage.

Usage and budget

We mentioned usage in the How to charge for your photography formula and a little bit about how it influences the price you ask. Apart from knowing for what your photograph is being used it is always good to know the budget your client is on, if he is on any. The budget can go from either extreme (low to high) to anywhere in between. There are two issues about the budget.

If the budget is high and you name your price very low you will not only be very affordable and cheap, you will also very probably be doubted as far as your experience and quality goes. Because, if you were better experienced and offered better quality, you would know to ask for more money. So, if the budget is high the most common practice is to match it, never go below. If you don't get the budget right away, my advice would be, if there is time and space to do that, ask for the budget and say you need to calculate the expenses and check some prices with gear rentals, etc. Then call back.

If the budget is low, you can not name a high price and expect that someone will raise the budget just because you say so. You can either accept the job or decline it. If you say you're doing it for a set amount of dollars you are probably giving another photographer a chance to make

42

some money even if he is maybe worse in quality than you are.

For example:

If you are shooting for a brochure of a company they will use to promote a product or just to promote the company and it prints in 3.000 copies, you could charge that job several thousand dollars. I'd say $2-3.000.

If, on the other hand, you are shooting for a magazine which prints almost a million copies and uses your photograph even in more than one issue of it you could probably charge around... drumroll, please... $300. This is where budget comes into play, but you'll need to console yourself that you are still getting references, connections and try to get credit for the photo too. Credit line won't feed you or pay your health insurance, it probably won't even get you clients, but it's a means to get to a consensus.

NEVER justify your price with your gear

For one, nobody wants to know what gear you are using when photographing them. Unless you are photographing another photographers wedding, they couldn't care less about your lenses and what you are doing as long as you are providing quality work.

And secondly, you may very well get a reaction that nobody is fault you wanted to buy a Hasselblad and shoot it, so your price automatically goes up. No, it doesn't.

Unlike some puritans would probably say, the gear actually is important, but it doesn't dictate your price (unless you're charging rentals). The new and better gear might very well get your job done faster and with more ease. It could even do it better, but you need to be responsive for that. The gear isn't working, you are. Your clients are not paying your gear by the hour, they are paying you. Or are you considering charging the fact you went to photography school and seminars also? If you want to price more, there are other ways to justify it, don't use the gear for that.

As photographers we usualy hate when someone says something like „Oh, that is a great camera, it must take great pictures". So, if that is the case, stop promoting the camera and take credit for those great pictures and charge for your time.

Knowing when to leave and doing so

Negotiating can lead you only so far and sometimes you just can not close the deal you maybe want. At this point you will probably want to introduce Michael Port's red velvet rope policy and keep the clients you don't want outside of it.

There are no exact instructions for this and, like art, there's no exact science about it. You need to guesstimate the point when you are not moving anywhere with your client. Once you do that you need to know your value, take a stand and leave. While trying to explain to a „hostile" client why and how you can do better and more than his uncle Bob you could have used that time to close a deal with another client, answer some e-mails, post some social media posts, spend time with your loved ones. In any way... walking aways every now and then is not only a good thing, it's necessary.

Photography contracts

No matter what kind of photography you are doing or if you are a beginner or already a seasoned photographer, you will need to have a contract in today's society to protect yourself and your business. Today everyone can get sued for everything (especially in the USA). So in order to prevent your grandchildren paying of your debt you really should take some time and get a contract. I have not tried it but Rocket Lawyer offers free custom draft of a photography contract.

Even if you are only doing fine art, not dealing with people or buildings – for people you always need a model release and for building you need a property release most of the time – you want to have a contract in case a gallery owner has interest for your work or you want to sell your print. For your and the clients safety everything needs to be put on paper, so in case of litigation you have proper evidence.

The problem photographers face with getting their clients to sign the contract is the fear of scaring the clients with a legal form. People are in general afraid of signing something they need to fulfil sometimes in the future and follow the rules they have agreed to because we never know what can happen, but for the society to be as safe as we can make it we agree to a certain level of that phobia, giving up a little bit of the comfort.

Myself, I like that the contract to be written in form of a bill or something, so it has a more 'law-y' look to it and it may look a little bit more professional and serious. I would personally suggest having this kind of contract, where you state that the photos will not be available to any third parties, but then have a clause that says „unless the client has agreed to it signing a model release, provided with the contract". For the model release I suggest you use those found on the microstock sites if you are going to use the photos for that. Also, there is an iOS and Android application iStock accepts and a model release, it's called Easy release. If you are not using the photos for microstock then you may want to change that clause in your contract or make a separate model release.

You will want to cover in your contract as much as possible. There is a possibility that if it's too long you might scare people off, but explain that it is for both of your best interest and they might change that fear to security. You want to know what your and your clients rights and duties are, who is getting the copyright, what is the product, what postprocessing do you offer with it and what is extra, your working hours, how long does it take to deliver the photographs, payment, how much, how, when, what if the client is late etc. How can the contract be canceled, how much in advance should it be, how can the images made be used, model release, property release etc. Other photographers and guests photographing can also be agreed upon. Some photographers will ask that they (and the possible associate) are the only photographer, some will ask that other photographers/guests retain from using flash, some will ask that no one is to bring a camera with interchangeable lenses. I have always found funny the meal clause, but if you consider your working day of 8 hours you will find that you need to eat. Also, the meal times is, apart from eating, also for going over some stuff with the client, backing up your photographs, etc. since not many people like to be photographed with their mouths open taking a bite. Always have one article to protect yourself – you are not fault if the guest damages your gear, or they push in front of you for the photograph etc. They can sue you only for the price they paid you. What happens in case of illness or something else.

Some clients will agree on all these and some will not like one article or one paragraph or several, but there is no need to write a complete new contract because of that. Build an exclusion clause in your contract and have a space reserved to write in hand what those exclusions are.

If you have a booking or a scheduling fee you might not want to refer to it as a deposit. In legal terms a deposit is something you leave to the provider of goods just to get classified as a serious customer. If the client goes through the deposit is deducted from the total cost. What if the client does not go through with it? The deposit may be refundable. While charging a fee for booking isn't.

DMCA takedown notice

Most of us know that we keep our copyright from the second we shoot something untill we sell it to someone, unless there is a contract where we shoot for an employer and the copyright goes automatically to him, which kind of goes under the „untill we sell it" part. We also know that we can sue a person for infringement and get money.

Using the advantages of this notice you can, if you so choose, after you try to reason with the person who infringed you, send this notice to the online service provider or internet service provider. Basically, you go and tell on the infringer to someone higher than him and say „This person infringed me, here are the screenshots of the site and my pictures to prove my copyright, take his site down" and the service provider goes „OK". So, next time the infringer or someone else trying to open his site types in the address he gets greeted by the black screen of death.

The "DMCA take down notice" is a creature of Title II of the Digital Millennium Copyright Act. It added Section 512 to Title 17 of the United States Code, which basically exempts certain online service providers from liability for copyright infringing acts by its users, provided it meets certain conditions (such as being responsive to copyright holders when given notice of infringement on the network the OSP controls). When an OSP receives such a notice from a copyright holder, it is required to remove or disable access to the accused material in order to avoid being held liable itself. Complying with your request shields it from being held as a contributory or vicarious infringer if you're right about your claim. The DMCA also shields the OSP from liability to its customer if the material is held ultimately not to be infringing.

What type of content can be infringed on?
• Text (TXT, RTF, DOC, DOCx, PDF, PPT, PAGES, etc.)
• Images, pictures & photos (BMP, EPS, SVG, JPG, JPEG, GIF, PNG, PSD, RAW, TIFF, etc.)
• Video (MPG, AVI, RM, MOV, Quicktime, Windows Media Player, RealPlayer)
• Music & audio (AIF, AU, MP3, MP4, MID, WAV, etc.)
• Images found on Facebook, Tumblr, Pinterest, Flickr

How do you know who to contact?

You can use some web tools like whois.net or domaintools or any other tool you like for that purpose.

How do you know you're infringed?

Once you have a community online you could rely on your followers to let you know if they come across one or more of your work under another name. If you do not have that many or a larger variety of followers then you may want to use some tools to check on your images. One is google images. One other tool you might like as a photographer is a website called Tin Eye. It will search the internet for similar photographs and let you know where they appear.

The DMCA takedown notice will be of great help if the service provider is in the United States. Outside of the States it is likely to be ignored, but you should contact the provider anyway. Even if they do not have legal obligation to do so, they may do it under moral obligation or just the way they like to do business.

The DMCA takedown notice must:

• Be in writing.
• Contain your signature as the copyright owner.
• Identify the copyrighted work you claim has been infringed on. This can be done by identifying the work by title, or if it is more practical, you may consider providing a link to your website or other location where the work is being displayed lawfully. Some people also attach a copy of the copyright protected work to aid in the takedown. This is particularly helpful when dealing with photographs or other images.
• Identify the material that has infringed your work. You should include sufficient information to allow the copyright agent to identify where the infringing content is being made available without your permission.
• Include your contact information. E-mail address is sufficient.
• State that you complain in „good faith". A statement must be included in the letter that confirms you have good faith belief that use of the material in the manner described in the letter is not authorized by the copyright owner, or its licensing representatives.
• State that „under penalty of perjury, that the information contained in the notification is accurate". Providing false information and making a false claim is punishable under federal law, and those making false notices can be sued and held civilly liable.
• State that you have the right to proceed.

The content can also be removed from the search engines.

If you are held as an infringer by mistake and your website has been taken down, you can file a counter notice using the same pattern as filing the takedown notice.

51

If all this is a bit too much for you then you can also make use of services that do this for you. DMCA.com offers either professional services to do this or the tools the professionals use for you to do it yourself.

Quotes

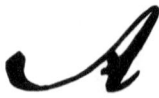

Aaron Sussman

ƒ Photography is a way of feeling, of touching, of loving. What you have caught on film is captured forever, it remembers little things, long after you have forgotten everything.

ƒ Photography is a means of recording forever the things one sees for a moment.

A. K. Nicholas

ƒ Keep shooting. It helps the model's confidence. Flashing strobes are like applause.

Abraham Lincoln

ƒ There are no bad pictures; that's just how your face looks sometimes.

Abigail Marie

ƒ Anyone can pick up a fancy camera and call themself a photographer, but those who can take the cheapest gadget and the most menial subject and make something beautiful from it are the true photographer.

Adriana Lestido

f I do not photograph what I see, because I already saw it. What I want to see is what my eyes can't see. I photograph what I feel but I cannot see.

Al Perry

f Whatever I lack in ability, I make up in equipment.

Alan Milan

f Photography for me is seeing the world not just merely looking at it.

Albert Einstein

f A photograph never grows old. You and I change, people change all through the months and years but a photograph always remains the same. How nice to look at a photograph of mother or father taken many years ago. You see them as you remember them. But as people live on, they change completely. That is why I think a photograph can be kind.

f Few are those who see with their own eyes and feel with their own hearts.

f Make things as simple as possible, but no simpler.

Albert Normandin

f You have to open your mind to your eyes.

f The difference between Art and Shit is someone's opinion.

Alec Soth

ƒ I fell in love with taking pictures, with wandering around finding things. To me it feels like a kind of performance. The picture is a document of that performance.

Alex Tehrani

ƒ Anyone can shoot chaos. But the most perceptive photographers can make compelling pictures out of uninteresting moments.

Alexander Rodchenko

ƒ Photography has all the rights, and all the merits, necessary for us to turn towards it as the art of our time.

Alexander Tsiaras

ƒ My responsibility as scientist and journalist is to provide accurate information. My desire as artist is to make the images beautiful.

Alexey Brodovitch

ƒ The pictures a mature photographer takes are interpretations of the subject in terms of the photographer's own personality and interests. If he has inventiveness, photography can be completely rediscovered in his own way.

ƒ When the novice photographer starts taking pictures, he carries his camera about and shoots everything that interests him. There comes a time when he must crystallize his ideas and set off in an particular direction. He must learn that shooting for the sake of shooting is dull and unprofitable.

ƒ The creative life of the commercial photographer is like the life of a butterfly. Very seldom do we see a photographer who is really productive for more than eight or ten years.

Alfred Eisenstaedt

ƒ When I have a camera in my hand, I know no fear.

ƒ Once the amateur's naive approach and humble willingness to learn fades away, the creative spirit of good photography dies with it. Every professional should remain always in his heart an amateur.

ƒ Never boss people around. It's more important to click with people than to click the shutter.

ƒ Retire? Retire from What? Life? I will only retire when I am dead and people will say 'that's the man who shot that picture of the sailor and the nurse on VJ Day' *(Victory over Japan Day op.a.)*!

ƒ I don't like to work with assistants. I'm already one too many; the camera alone would be enough.

ƒ In a photograph a person's eyes tell much, sometimes they tell all.

ƒ Keep it simple.

ƒ I expose longer. *(when asked what he did at night in Paris) ƒ* The important thing is not the camera but the eye.

Alfred Stieglitz

ƒ I do not object to retouching, dodging or accentuation as long as they do not interfere with the natural qualities of photographic technique.

ƒ In photography there is a reality so subtle that it becomes more real than reality.

ƒ Alfread Stieglitz was once asked: „How does a photographer learn?" He answered without even a second's hesitation: „By looking".

ƒ A shutter working at a speed of one-fourth to one-twenty-fifth of a second will answer all purposes. A little blur in a moving subject will often aid to giving the impression of action and motion.

ƒ I am not a painter, nor an artist. Therefore I can see straight, and that may be my undoing.

Alvin Langdon Coburn

ƒ A photographic portrait needs more collaboration between sitter and artist than a painted portrait.

Anaïs Nin

ƒ We don't see things as they are, we see them as we are.

Andre Bazin

ƒ Photography does not create eternity, as art does; it embalms time, rescuing it simply from its proper corruption.

Andre Kertesz

ƒ Seeing is not enough; you have to feel what you photograph.

ƒ Mr. Kertesz was known for his drive and enthusiasm. At 90, he produced a portfolio of new pictures and showed it to the photographer Susan May Tell. When she asked him what it was that kept him working, he replied, „I am still hungry.“

Andrew Stark

ƒ My work is nothing more than the visual diary of a very long walk.

Andreas Feininger

ƒ Unless a subject intrest me, I'll pass it over and save my film for better things.

ƒ Before you shoot an irrestible subject, mute all your senses except sight to find out how much is left for the camera to record.

ƒ *Know–how* is worthless unless guided by *know–why* and *know–when*.

ƒ A technically perfect photograph can be the world's most boring picture.

f As an amateur you have an advantage over photographers – you can do as you wish. This should make amateurs the happiest of photographers.

Andrew Vachss

f It all comes down to the same thing. You can't make anything happen, you just have to be ready when it does.

Andri Cauldwell

f To see in color is a delight for the eye but to see in black and white is a delight for the soul.

f Photography is an art form like no other. It allows you to instantaneously capture time, and at the same moment, fade the colors of day into night so that you can print them out again and give them to the world, in the purity of black and white.

Andy Greaves

f You can't reproduce nature with a photograph or a painting. You can only honour it.

Andy Warhol

f My idea of a good picture is one that's in focus and of a famous person.

f Photographers feel guilty that all they do for a living is press a button.

f Art is what you can get away with.

ƒ An artist is somebody who produces things that people don't need to have.

ƒ I just do art because I'm ugly and there's nothing else for me to do.

ƒ You know it's art, when the check clears.

Anne Geddes

ƒ The best images are the ones that retain their strength and impact over the years, regardless of the number of times they are viewed.

ƒ The hardest thing in photography is to create a simple image.

Anne Tucker

ƒ All art requires courage.

Annie Leibovitz

ƒ Computer photography won't be photography as we know it. I think photography will always be chemical.

ƒ A thing that you see in my pictures is that I was not afraid to fall in love with these people.

ƒ Sometimes I enjoy just photographing the surface because I think it can be as revealing as going to the heart of the matter.

ƒ One doesn't stop seeing. One doesn't stop framing. It doesn't turn off and turn on. It's on all the time.

Annie Lennox

ƒ For me, pointing and clicking my phone is absolutely fine. People say that isn't the art of photography but I don't agree.

Ansel Adams

ƒ There are no rules for good photographs, there are only good photographs.

ƒ Landscape photography is the supreme test of the photographer – and often the supreme disappointment.

ƒ You don't take a photograph, you make it.

ƒ A good photograph is knowing where to stand.

ƒ The single most important component of a camera is the twelve inches behind it.

ƒ When words become unclear, I shall focus with photographs. When images become inadequate, I shall be content with silence.

ƒ To the complaint, „There are no people in these photographs", I respond, „There are always two people: the photographer and the viewer".

ƒ Sometimes I arrive just when God's ready to have somone click the shutter.

ƒ A photograph is usually looked at- seldom looked into.

ƒ There is nothing worse than a sharp image of a fuzzy concept.

ƒ Dodging and burning are steps to take care of mistakes God made in establishing tonal relationships.

ƒ Twelve significant photographs in any one year is a good crop.

ƒ A true photograph need not be explained, nor can it be contained in words.

ƒ The term accessories has come to include a host of photographic gadgets of questionable value.

ƒ A photograph is not an accident, it is a concept.

ƒ Life is your art. An open, aware heart is your camera. A oneness with your world is your film. Your bright eyes and easy smile is your museum.

ƒ It is horrifying that we have to fight our own government to save the environment.

ƒ Chance favors the prepared mind.

Antoine D'Agata

ƒ It's not how a photographer looks at the world that is important. It's their intimate relationship with it.

Antoine de Saint-Exupéry

ƒ It is only with the heart that one can see rightly, what is essential is invisible to the eye.

Amy Arbus

𝑓 When I ask to photograph someone, it is because I love the way they look and I think I make that clear. I'm paying them a tremendous compliment. What I'm saying is, I want to take you home with me and look at you for the rest of my life.

April Aldighieri

𝑓 No photo left behind.

April Saul

𝑓 Some photojournalists talk about being a fly on the wall when shooting. I really don't accept that. You have to give of yourself for your subjects to give something back.

Aristotle

𝑓 You should never think without an image.

𝑓 The soul can not think without a picture.

Arnold Newman

𝑓 A lot of photographers think that if they buy a better camera they'll be able to take better photographs. A better camera won't do a thing for you if you don't have anything in your head or in your heart.

𝑓 The photographer must be a part of the picture.

ƒ We don't take pictures with our cameras. We take them with our hearts and we take them with our minds, and the camera is nothing more than a tool.

Arthur Meyerson

ƒ I'm a photoholic! I love photography. I love taking photographs. I love looking at photographs. And, some of my best friends are photographers.

Arthur Rothstein

ƒ It is a rare photographer who can take a detached, cold-blooded view of his work.

Arturo Macias Uceda

ƒ In all my best photos I always claim that I was behind the camera and in all my bad ones I always maintain that my camera was in front of me.

ƒ In all my photos, I always got at least one person that closed an eye and usually it is me.

ƒ If you don't know the difference (between a good or an average photo) you won't see the difference.

ƒ I think God created the World based on photograph he saw in a magazine.

Astor Morgan

ƒ I am not impressed by the number of mediocre images your new camera shoots in one second.

August Sander

f In photography there are no shadows that cannot be illuminated.

f Photography has no dark sides!

f I never made a person look bad. They do that themselves. The portrait is your mirror. It's you.

B

Ben Shahn

f It may be a point of great pride to have a Van Gogh on the living room wall, but the prospects of having Van Gogh himself in the living room would put a great many devoted art lovers to rout.

f An amateur is an artist who supports himself with outside jobs which enable him to paint. A professional is someone whose wife works to enable him to paint.

Berenice Abott

f Photography can never grow up if it imitates some other medium. It has to walk alone; it has to be itself.

f Photography helps people to see.

f People say they need to express their emotions – I'm sick of that. Photography doesn't teach you to express your emotions it teachs you to see.

f There are many teachers who could ruin you. Before you know it you could be a pale copy of this teacher or that teacher. You have to evolve on your own.

f Abstraction in photography is ridiculous, and is only an imitation of painting. We stopped imitating painters a hundred years ago, so to imitate them in this day and age is laughable.

f I agree that all good photographs are documents, but I also know that all documents are certainly not good photographs. Furthermore, a good photographer does not merely document, he probes the subject, he "uncovers" it.

Bertolt Brecht

f Photography has become a formidable weapon against truth in the hands of the bourgeoisie. The enormous quantity of picture material spit out daily by the printing press, that consequently appears to possess the character of truth, actually serves only to obscure the facts. The camera can lie just like the type-setting machine.

Bill Brandt

f I am not interested in rules or conventions. Photography is not a sport.

f A good nude photograph can be erotic, but certainly not sentimental or pornographic.

Bill Burt

f A good color image is a good black and white image.

Bill Cunningham

f The main thing I love about street photography is that you find the answers you don't see at the fashion shows. You find information for readers so they can visualize themselves.

Bill Frakes

f You should make photographs with your heart, mind, eye and soul. The capture device is simply there to allow you to transfer your vision to a medium that you can share with others.

Bill Horan

f My best shot on a 36 exposure roll seems to be on the 37th frame.

Bill Jay

f Evolution in action: First, God said, „Let there be light". Then, he created two nude models. Now we have photographers.

f Photoshop makes it easier to do all the things you didn't need to do before Photoshop.

f At exhibition openings always praise the chicken for laying eggs; you can wring its neck later.

f Ask photographers to write and they have nothing to say; ask them to talk about their work and they won't shut up.

f Advice to artists: always take the opportunity to shut up.

f „I am a camera" but it is a discontinued model.

ƒ I start a lot of photo projects but never seem to...

Bill Owens

ƒ Working forty hours a week for a large newspaper leaves one with little time to develop one's own ideas or picture stories. A news photographer can become so busy that he has no time to do photography.

ƒ

When someone sees me with a camera that weights almost ten pounds, he assumes immediately that I'm a serious photographer.

Bill Stettner

ƒ When a 20 year old advertising art director doesn't know the difference between a good picture and a bad picture, and keeps insisting it's 'good enough', it's hard for me to keep working as a photographer.

ƒ I won't do cigarette shots anymore even though I once made $500,000 a year from Reynolds tobacco. I won't sell my soul. I can't put up with the deceit and ignorance from advertising agencies. I just can't do it.

Bob Kirst

ƒ Carrying a camera on vacation pretty much guarantees you won't see anything worth shooting.

Brassai

ƒ Do you know what Picasso said when he looked at my drawings in 1939? "You're crazy, Brassai. You have a gold mine and you spend your time exploiting a salt mine!" The salt mine was – naturally – photography!

f To keep from going stale you must forget your professional outlook and rediscover the virginal eye of the amateur.

f To me photography must suggest, not insist or explain.

Bret Weston

f People are under the illusion that it's easy...Technically, it is complex. You have a million options with equipment to distract you. I tell my students to simplify their equipment.

f The taint of age can be very beautiful. The wreckage of man-made objects is something more beautiful than the new. Rust and weathering adds a patina of... well, I call it „elegant shit" or „elegant gorp".

Brigitte Bardot

f A photograph can be an instant of life captured for eternity that will never cease looking back at you.

Brooke Jensen

f Photography must ask the great questions of life, which ultimately does not include, „Which camera did you use"?

Brooks Atkinson

f The virtue of the camera is not the power it has to transform the photographer into an artist, but the impulse it gives him to keep on looking.

Bruce Gilden

f I love the people I photograph. I mean, they're my friends. I've never met most of them or I don't know them at all, yet through my images I live with them.

f If you can smell the street by looking at the photo, it's a street photograph.

f I'm known for taking pictures very close, and the older I get, the closer I get.

Bruno Barbey

f Photography is the only language that can be understood anywhere in the world.

Bruno Schreck

f Photographic success is not just about getting the equipment. And you can't market yourself without a portfolio. If you love photography enough, the equipment will come, the portfolio will result and if you enjoy the process, success will follow. You will evolve your own „formula".

Bryan Peterson

f First and foremost, make it an obvious picture of color! Rather than looking for rocks, leaves, trees, waterfalls, birds, flowers, fire hydrants, starfish, boats, orchards, or bridges, focus your energy and vision on red, blue, yellow, orange, green, or violet. Color first, content second!

ƒ There is no better time to crop a bad composition than just before you press the shutter release.

Burk Uzzle

ƒ Photography is a love affair with life.

Calvin Trilling

f The immature artist imitates; the mature artist steals.

Cameron Lawson

f I would come home from a climbing expedition and find it hard to describe the experience and beauty to my friends and family. Photography allowed me the vehicle to tell the visual story.

Caroline Mueller

f What I look for in pictures I take: eyes, hands, head tilt, body language, background and use of space.

Carl Bower

f As a photographer, I'm primarily interested in things I can't see.

Carl Mydans

f One is not really a photographer until preoccupation with learning has been outgrown and the camera in his hands is an extension of himself. There is where creativity begins.

Catherine Jo Morgan

ƒ A pro only means you shoot for pay. As an amateur, I learned from pros. As a pro, I continue to learn from amateurs.

ƒ The good work goes in the album; the bad work winds up on the passport

ƒ The progress of a photographer can often be marked by the accumulated number of mistake he or she had made along the way.

Charis Wilson

ƒ Edward Weston and I both agreed with the view of a Greek friend of ours, Jean Varda, who was fond of saying there were three perfect shapes in the world: the hull of a boat, a violin and a woman's body.

Charles Baudelaire

ƒ Photographers, you will never become artists. All you are is mere copiers.

Charles H. Caffin

ƒ There are two distinct roads in photography -- the utilitarian and the aesthetic, the goal of the one being a record of facts, and the other an expression of beauty.

Charles Moore

ƒ Pictures can and do make a difference.

Charles H. Traub

From: "The Dos and Don'ts of Graduate Studies: Maxims from the Chair" -- For years, Charles H. Traub (editor of "The Education of a Photographer") has willed these maxims upon his students. They were inspired by those of his own teacher, the cantankerous Arthur Siegel, at the Institute of Design.

ƒ   The Dos:

- o   Do something old in a new way.
- o   Do something new in an old way.
- o   Do something new in a new way; whatever works, works.
- o   Do it sharp – if you can't, call it art.
- o   Do it in the computer – if it can be done there.
- o   Do fifty of them – you will definitely get a show.
- o   Do it big – if you can't do it big, do it red.
- o   If all else fails, turn it upside down – if it looks good, it might work.
- o   Do bend your knees.
- o   If you don't know what to do, look up or down – but continue looking.
- o   Do celebrities – if you do a lot of them, you'll get a book.
- o   Connect with others – network.
- o   Edit it yourself.
- o   Design it yourself.
- o   Edit – when in doubt, shoot more.
- o   Edit again.
- o   Read Darwin, Marx, Joyce, Freud, Einstein, Benjamin, McLuhan, and Barthes.
- o   See Citizen Kane ten times.
- o   Look at everything – stare.

- Construct your images from the edge inward.
- If it's the 'real world,' do it in color.
- If it can be done digitally, do it.

ƒ The Don'ts:

- Don't do it about yourself – of your friend – or your family.
- Don't dare photograph yourself nude.
- Don't look at old family albums.
- Don't hand-color it.
- Don't write on it.
- Don't use alternative processes – if it ain't straight, do it in the computer.
- Don't gild the lily – a.k.a. less is more.
- Don't go to video when you don't know what else to do.
- Don't photograph indigent people, particularly in foreign lands.
- Don't whine, just produce.

Charles Harbut

ƒ A photograph is a collision between a person with a camera and reality. The photograph is typically as interesting as the collision is.

Chase Jarvis

ƒ The best camera is the one that's with you.

ƒ Be different, not better.

ƒ You have to be zig-ing when people are zag-ing.

f Having learned it once I feel realy comfortable saying „I don't know". If I was to give any advice it would be to be comfortable not knowing. And it's when you're trying to pretend you know something you don't know – it's when mistakes happen.

Chris Niedenthal

f The Evil is always more photogenic than the Good.

Christopher Isherwood

f I am a camera with its shutter open, quite passive, recording, not thinking.

Cindy Sherman

f People think because it's photography it's not worth as much, and because it's a woman artist, you're still not getting as much – there's still definitely that happening. I'm still really competitive when it comes to, I guess, the male painters and male artists. I still think that's really unfair.

Cliff Hollenbeck

f You don't have to be crazy to succeed as a photographer, but it sure helps. It's okay to be crazy, but not stupid.

f Faith in your photographic abilities is the willingness to venture into darkness without a flash.

Clyde Butcher

ƒ I've been pursuing the concept of wilderness preservation since 1961. I think it's important for an artist to have a passion—you need to find a source of inspiration.

Clyde McConnell

ƒ Photography is a vale of tears.

Coco J. Ginger

ƒ Life is wonderful when you're the one to write it.

Confucius

ƒ Everything has it's beauty, but not everyone sees it.

Conrad Hall

ƒ Contrast is what makes photography interesting.

Courtney Milne

ƒ Those who find beauty in a landscape do so because it touches a place of beauty already within themselves.

Craig Coverdale

ƒ There are things hidden for all the world until photographed.

f   Street photography is a renewable resource. If you dont like what you see wait 5 minutes or walk a hundred feet.

f   Remember, not everything is a picture. A good eye can edit before the shutter opens.

Christophe Agou

f   Looking and seeing are two different things. What matters is the relationship with the subject

f   The road from the eye to the heart is easy to follow. I am taking it with my eyes closed.

f   The distance between yourself and others should not be greater than your arm's length.

Dara McGrath

f Photography is an itch that wont go away. No matter how much you scratch it.

Dan Burge

f You don't want to store prints in an attic or basement, or in a humid or hot environment. Generally the rule of thumb is if you're comfortable, the photographs are too.

Dan Chung

f Don't rush it. Take your time. Compose.

Daniel Rubinstein

f The photographer should suffer, not the audience.

Danny Gregory

f Please do waste art materials. Use paper. Empty paint jars. Deplete pens. If it's teaching you stuff, it's not being wasted.

David Acuna

f Your mind is like a live camera that is constantly taking pictures of every single moment that comes onto you. So be a good photographer!

David Alan Harvey

ƒ Don't shoot what it looks like. Shoot what it feels like.

David Bailey

ƒ It takes a lot of imagination to be a good photographer. You need less imagination to be a painter because you can invent things. But in photography everything is so ordinary; it takes a lot of looking before you learn to see the extraordinary.

ƒ Everyone will take one great picture, I've done better because I've taken two.

ƒ When I die I want to go to Vogue.

David Burnett

ƒ The satisfaction comes from working next to 500 photographers and coming away with something different.

ƒ You are in a perfectly bad mood until you can look through your viewfinder and see that meaningful moment.

ƒ The eye and the brain react to the foreign, so when you are shooting in the same place for a long time, you really have to push yourself beyond autopilot.

ƒ The greatest photographs are motivated by human feeling.

David Hockney

ƒ I've finally figured out what's wrong with photography. It's a one-eyed man looking through a little 'ole. Now, how much reality can there be in that?

ƒ There is nothing wrong with photography, if you don't mind the perspective of a paralysed Cyclops.

David Huffines

ƒ Photography is capturing life's moments every 1/100 of a second.

ƒ When photographing, turn around, your best picture might be behind you.

ƒ Do you control the camera or does the camera control you? If you're not shooting on manual mode, you are nothing but a human tripod!

ƒ Photography is one of the most advanced art forms, yet it is the most unappreciated.

David Lee Roth

ƒ There's no such thing as a bad picture, you just look bad.

David P

ƒ Green mode (auto) is for when you hand your camera to somebody to take a picture of you.

David Richardson

ƒ I have always photographed loneliness because that is my life.

David Ward

ƒ A great photograph is a distillation, a reduction of the chaos of our wider experience to a visually satisfying essence where what is excluded is as important as what is included.

David Winge

ƒ Putting clothes on a model is akin to putting a parking lot over a field of flowers.

Davor Pavlić

ƒ To the question „What is the goal of doing photography?" – „Like any other kind of art. Express yourself, interest others, leave a trace, live forever."

ƒ If it has an M mode, it's a pro camera. I am tired of people making excuses they have a bad camera and all they know is how to turn it on and off.

ƒ There is something about black and white that is simple, but strong, something that draws in the soul instead of the eye.

Dean Collins

ƒ Beauty is in the eye of the checkbook holder.

Dennis Hopper

f   Like all artists I want to cheat death a little and contribute something to the next generation.

Diane Arbus

f   I always thought of photography as a naughty thing to do – that was one of my favourite things about it, and when I first did it, I felt very perverse.

f   I never have taken a picture I've intended. They're always better or worse.

f   Regardless of how you feel inside, always try to look like a winner. Even if you are behind, a sustained look of control and confidence can give you a mental edge that results in victory.

f   One of the risks of appearing in public is the likelihood of being photographed.

f   I tend to think of the act of photographing, generally speaking, as an adventure. My favorite thing is to go where I've never been.

f   I really believe there are things nobody would see if I didn't photograph them.

f   Lately I've been struck with how I really love what you can't see in a photograph.

f   Taking pictures is like tiptoeing into the kitchen late at night and stealing Oreo cookies.

Dick Bruna

ƒ If you put very few things on a page, you leave lots of room for imagination.

Didier Lefevr

ƒ Taking a good photo is a real struggle. It's a mistake to think that you'll get good photos just by going to a war.

Dieter Appelt

ƒ A snapshot steals life that it cannot return. A long exposure (creates) a form that never existed.

Dominic Rouse

ƒ To see the light we must first acknowledge that we are in the dark.

ƒ Colour is everything, black and white is more.

ƒ Art is the exploration of the human mind by the human mind.

ƒ We should not be photographing people because they are famous but because they are human.

ƒ I sometimes wish that I could paint badly. There appears to be money in it.

Don Doll

ƒ For me photography is a form of prayer.

Dorothea Lange

ƒ Photography takes an instant out of time, altering life by holding it still.

ƒ Pick a theme and work it to exhaustion... the subject must be something you truly love or truly hate.

ƒ The camera is an instrument that teaches people how to see without a camera.

ƒ You know, so often it's just sticking around and being there, remaining there, not swooping out in a cloud of dust: sitting down on the ground with people, letting children look at your camera with their dirty, grimy little hands, and putting their fingers on the lens, and you just let them, because you know that if you will behave in a generous manner, you are apt to receive it, you know?

ƒ Photographers stop photographing a subject too soon before they have exhausted the possibilities.

ƒ Hands off! I do not molest what I photograph, I do not meddle and I do not arrange.

ƒ I would like to see photographers become responsible and photography realize its potential.

ƒ One should really use the camera as though tomorrow you'd be stricken blind. To live a visual life is an enormous undertaking, practically unattainable. I have only touched it, just touched it.

f I realize more and more what it takes to be a really good photographer. You go in over your head, not just up to your neck.

f My own approach is based upon three considerations. First – hands off ! Whenever I photograph I do not molest or tamper with or arrange. Second – a sense of place. I try to picture as part of its surroundings, as having roots. Third – a sense of time. Whatever I photograph, I try to show as having its position in the past or in the present.

Dorothy Bohm

f The most important thing for a photographer is to get consistency of good woork. Anyone can take a good photograph – but doing it consistently is the problem.

Doug Menuez

f Photography is my passion. It's more then a profession to me. It's my obsession. Whether on assignment or off asignment, I always have to have my camera with me. You never know when you're gonna see a picture.

f I love to walk the streets hunting for pictures, for moments.

f I prefer if I have a smaler camera. Then I'm not signaling my presence and I can more easily find real moments.

f 28mm. It's perfect for street photography. It forces you to step in and be intimate with your subjects. And if you take a step back you see their whole environment.

f Every picture to me is a gift.

f By carefuly arranging objects you can find a visual poetry in any ordinary subject.

f I don't separate what I do on assignments from what I do for myself. I'm always seeing.

Drew Carey

f Being a celebrity you always get really good seats to sporting events but you never get as good seats as the photographers get. And I really love sports. So one of the scams I have going now is I want to learn sports photography so I can get better seats at a sporting event.

Duane Michals

f Trust that little voice in your head that says „Wouldn't it be interesting if..." and then do it.

f And in not learning the rules, I was free. I always say, you're either defined by the medium or you redefine the medium in terms of your needs.

f A photograph of a woman crying tells me nothing about grief. Or a photograph of a woman ecstatic tells me nothing about ecstasy. What is the nature of these emotions? The problem with photography is that it only deals with appearances.

Eddie Adams

ƒ Still photographs are the most powerful weapon in the world. People believe them, but photographs do lie, even without manipulation. They are only half-truths.

Eddie Soloway

ƒ If you ever need a coach, someone to show you the way, bring along a kid. What he sees will lead you to all sorts of imaging adventures.

Edgar Degas

ƒ Daylight is too easy. What I want is difficult - the atmosphere of lamps and moonlight.

ƒ Art is not what you see, but what you make others see.

Edmond Terakopian

ƒ Humanity is the foundation of any image. Then comes the journalism aspect, and then the photography.

ƒ Its not your story, it belongs to your subject. You must never forget that.

Edouard Boubat

f There are certain pictures I can never take. We turn on the TV and are smothered with cruelty and suffering and I don't need to add to it. So I just photograph peaceful things. A vase of flowers, a beautiful girl. Sometimes, through a peaceful face, I can bring something important into the world.

Edsel Adams

f The restless photographer never seems to have enough equipment.

Edward Abbey

f Our job is to record, each in his own way, this world of light and shadow and time that will never come again exactly as it is today.

Edward K. Thompson

f Don't tell me about the pictures you didn't get. Just show me the good ones you got.

Edward Steichen

f A portrait is not made in the camera but on either side of it.

f Once you really commence to see things, then you really commence to feel things.

ƒ Every other artist begins with a blank canvas, a piece of paper... the photographer begins with the finished product.

ƒ Photography is a major force in explaining man to man.

Edward Weston

ƒ Photography to the amateur is recreation, to the professional it is work, and hard work too, no matter how pleasurable it my be.

ƒ To consult the rules of composition before making a picture is a little like consulting the law of gravitation before going for a walk.

ƒ If I have any „message" worth giving to a beginner it is that there are no short cuts in photography.

ƒ Anything more than 500 yards from the car just isn't photogenic.

ƒ Ultimately success or failure in photographing people depends on the photographer's ability to understand his fellow man.

ƒ I don't care if you make a print on a bath mat, just as long as it is a good print.

Eliot Elisofon

ƒ Most people try to include too much in the picture. If you are photographing a child playing on the lawn, photograph the child, not the trees, the house, and everything else in sight. Photography is really a simple statement and the clearer it is the better.

Eliot Porter

ƒ The more you photograph, the more you realize what can and what can't be photographed. You just have to keep doing it.

ƒ Photography is a strong tool, a propaganda device, and a weapon for the defense of the environment and therefore for the fostering of a healthy human race and even very likely for its survival.

ƒ Sometimes you can tell a large story with a tiny subject.

Elliott Erwitt

ƒ To me, photography is an art of observation. It's about finding something interesting an ordinary place... I've found it has little to do with the things you see and everything to do with the way you see them.

ƒ All the technique in the world doesn't compensate for the inability to notice.

ƒ I like things that have to do with what is real, elegant, well presented and without excessive style. In other words, just fine observetion.

ƒ Photography is a craft. Anyone can learn a craft with normal intelligence and application. To take it beyond the craft is something else. That's when magic comes in. And I don't know that there's any explanation for that.

ƒ After following the crowd for a while, I'd then go 180 degrees in the exact opposite direction. It always worked for me, but then again, I'm very lucky.

Ellis Vener

ƒ Technical perfection is not the goal of photography: seeing life is.

Elizabeth Metcalf

ƒ The rarest thing in the world is a woman who is pleased with photograph of herself.

Emile Zola

ƒ In my view you cannot claim to have seen something until you have photographed it.

ƒ If you ask me what I came to do in this world, I, an artist, will answer you: I am here to live out loud.

Eric Rossi

ƒ Learn the rules of photography in depth, then learn how you can break them to accomplish your vision.

ƒ As a photographer you have the power to capture a moment that no one else can.

Ernst Haas

ƒ There is only you and your camera. The limitations in your photography are in yourself, for what we see is what we are.

ƒ With photography a new language has been created. Now for the first time it is possible to express reality by reality. We can look at an impression as long as we wish, we can delve into it and, so to speak, renew past experiences at will.

ƒ Best wide-angle lens? Two steps backward. Look for the „ah-ha".

ƒ The camera doesn't make a bit of difference. All of them can record what you are seeing. But, you have to see.

ƒ I am not interested in shooting new things - I am interested to see things new.

ƒ A picture is the expression of an impression. If the beautiful were not in us, how would we ever recognize it?

ƒ Don't torture yourself with too much equipment. It will tire you and cripple your concentration.

ƒ If art is aristocratic, photography is its democratic voice.

Estelle Jussim

ƒ If you greatly admire many of Edward Weston's photographs – as I do – and if you find them aesthetically majestic, recognize their substantial influence and their high status in contemporary criticism, you may turn to the photographer's writings in an effort to discover his intentions, his philosophies, perhaps even his secrets. Expect complexity.

Eugene Delacroix

ƒ If a man of genius uses daguerreotype as it ought to be used, he will raise himself to heights unknown to us.

ƒ As far as I am concerned, I can only say how much I regret such an admirable discovery should have come so late. The possibility of studying such images would have had an influence on me that I can only guess at from the usefulness which they have now, even in the little time left me for more intensive study. It is the tangible proof of nature's own design, which we otherwise see only very feebly.

Evan Clarke

ƒ When you start showing your work to others, the purity of the art diminishes. You do pure art for yourself.

Eve Arnold

ƒ If the photographer is interested in the people in front of his lens, and if he is compassionate, it's already a lot. The instrument is not the camera but the photographer.

ƒ I think if I ever get satisfied, I'll have to stop. It's the frustration that drives you.

Ewlises Gonzalez

ƒ To me photography is not a contest, it's my life.. so don't bother challenging me, I already won!

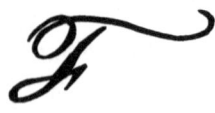

Faul Bosman

f Digital photography is doing for photography what the piano did for keyboard music.

Ferdinando Scianna

f A photograph is not created by a photographer. What they do is just to open a little window and capture it. The world then writes itself on the film. The act of the photographer is closer to reading than it is to writing. They are the readers of the world.

Francis Bacon

f The best part of beauty is that which no picture can express.

f Jesus would have been one of the best photographers that ever existed. He was always looking at the beauty of people souls. In fact Jesus was constantly making pictures of God in people's life by looking at their souls and exposing them to his light.

Frank Horvat

f Photography is the art of not pushing the button.

f The reason for holding back is not only to spare some film - it's like storing my energy, or rather my expectation; it's letting the image I want take shape in my mind, by the very act of refusing the images I don't want.

ƒ Taking a photograph is like responding to an appeal; as if a person, or a tree, or a situation was calling me, crying out to me „I wish to be made visible, and you are the one who can best do it".

Frank Jay Haynes

ƒ It pays to get the best lens you can afford.

ƒ All amateurs think they have to have the sun at their backs. You'll find this is wrong: If you get the sun to one side and catch the shadows, you get a 'Rembrandt-lighted' picture with good contrasts.

Frank Karycinski

ƒ Photoshop – that which produces a great photograph from an average photographer.

Frank Zappa

ƒ Art is making something out of nothing, and selling it.

Fred Burrell

ƒ Our eyes do not always work right. Minds are not corrected by optometrists. Often, what is most important to us is blurred by emotion and intensity of reaction.

Freddie Mercury

f Modern paintings are like women, you'll never enjoy them if you try to understand them.

Freeman Patterson

f The camera always points both ways. In expressing your subject, you also express yourself.

f 36 satisfactory exposures on a roll means a photographer is not trying anything new.

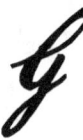

Galen Rowell

ƒ A lot of people think that when you have grand scenery, such as you have in Yosemite, that photography must be easy.

ƒ I think landscape photography in general is somewhat undervalued.

ƒ There is no question that photography has played a major role in the environmental movement.

ƒ I almost never set out to photograph a landscape, nor do I think of my camera as a means of recording a mountain or an animal unless I absolutely need a „record shot". My first thought is always of light.

ƒ You only get one sunrise and one sunset a day, and you only get so many days on the planet. A good photographer does the math and doesn't waste either.

Garry Winogrand

ƒ Photography is about finding out what can happen in the frame. When you put four edges around some facts, you change those facts.

ƒ If I saw something in my viewfinder that looked familiar to me, I would do something to shake it up.

ƒ Photographers mistake the emotion they feel while taking the photo as a judgment that the photograph is good.

ƒ No one moment is most important. Any moment can be something.

George Bernard Shaw

ƒ I've posed nude for a photographer in the manner of Rodin's Thinker, but I merely looked constipated.

ƒ If Velasquez were born today, he would be a photographer and not a painter.

ƒ Technically good negatives are more often the result of the survival of the fittest than of special creation: the photographer is like the cod, which lays a million eggs in order that one may reach maturity.

ƒ Some see things the way they are and ask, "Why?" I dream of things that never were, and ask "Why not?"

ƒ Though we have hundreds of photographs of Charles Dickens and Richard Wagner, we see nothing of them except the suits of clothes with their heads sticking out; and what is the use of that?

ƒ I would willingly exchange every single painting of Christ for one snapshot.

George Carlin

ƒ I don't own a camera, so I travel with a police sketch artist.

George Eastman

ƒ Light makes photography. Embrace light. Admire it. Love it. But above all, know light. Know it for all you are worth, and you will know the key to photography.

George Lottermoser

ƒ To photograph is to arrange elements within a defined space and capture that composition within a fragment of time.

ƒ Some photographers will emulate the masters and never achieve the masterpiece because the imitator's voice is not the master's voice. We must all find our own voice.

George Tice

ƒ As I progressed further with my project, it became obvious that it was really unimportant where I chose to photograph. The particular place simply provided an excuse to produce work... you can only see what you are ready to see - what mirrors your mind at that particular time.

Gerardo Suter

ƒ I didn't choose photography. Photography chose me.

Gertrude Käsebier

ƒ The key to artistic photography is to work out your own thoughts, by yourselves. Imitation leads to certain disaster.

Gianni Berengo Gardin

ƒ My artistic eye is black and white. I'm used to seeing and visualizing in black and white and have only one way of taking pictures.

Gilles Peress

ƒ I don't care so much anymore about „good photography", I am gathering evidence for history

ƒ I don't trust words. I trust pictures.

ƒ Every picture I take is like a diary entry.

Graciela Iturbide

ƒ The unconscious obsession that we photographers have is that wherever we go we want to find the theme that we carry inside ourselves.

Graeme Le Saux

ƒ The problem for me is that I've never actually studied photography, so it's quite a steep learning curve. Cameras these days do so much for you automatically but I still think there's a point where you should actually know the technical side.

Gustave Le Gray

ƒ A photograph is not created by a photographer. What they do is just to open a little window and capture it. The world then writes itself on the film. The act of the photographer is closer to reading than it is to writing. They are the readers of the world.

Guy Le Querrec

f A photographer is an acrobat treading the high wire of chance, trying to capture shooting stars.

f Taking pictures forces me to be more curious about life.

Guy Tal

f In the history of art, the sole reliance on being "different" or "original" had long been the crutch of the untalented.

f The mountains standing tall, clad in lush forests and adorned with snowy caps, inspire me like the beauty of a sensual woman dressed in her evening gown and finest jewelry. The deserts on the other hand lure me like the same woman standing naked in the sun.

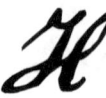

Harold Feinstein

f   When your mouth drops open, click the shutter.

Harry Callahan

f   I guess I've shot about 40,000 negatives and of these I have about 800 pictures I like.

f   I do believe strongly in photography and hope by following it intuitively that when the photographs are looked at they will touch the spirit in people.

f   I think nearly every artist continually wants to reach the edge of nothingness - the point where you can't go any further.

f   The mystery isn't in the technique, it's in each of us.

f   To be a photographer, one must photograph. No amount of book learning, no checklist of seminars attended, can substitute for the simple act of making pictures. Experience is the best teacher of all. And for that, there are no guarantees that one will become an artist. Only the journey matters.

Helmut Newton

f   My job as a portrait photographer is to seduce, amuse and entertain.

ƒ The first 10.000 shots are the worst. *(Similar: Henri Cartier-Bresson)*

ƒ In my vocabulary there are two bad words: art and good taste.

Henri Cartier-Bresson

ƒ In photography, the smallest thing can be a great subject. The little, human detail can become a Leitmotiv.

ƒ Of course it's all luck.

ƒ Your first 10.000 photographs are your worst. *(Similar: Helmut Newton)*

ƒ When the subject is in any way uneasy, the personality goes away where the camera can't reach it.

ƒ It is the photo that takes you; one must not take photos.

ƒ Sharpness is a bourgeois concept.

ƒ Impolite... like coming to a concert with a pistol in your hand. *(when expressing his views on the use of flash in photography.)*

ƒ Photography has not changed since its origin except in its technical aspects, which for me are not important.

ƒ Photography appears to be an easy activity; in fact it is a varied and ambiguous process in which the only common denominator among its practitioners is in the instrument.

ƒ The most difficult thing for me is a portrait. You have to try and put your camera between the skin of a person and his shirt.

ƒ And no photographs taken with the aid of flash light, either, if only out of respect for the actual light - even when there isn't any of it.

ƒ In a portrait, I'm looking for the silence in somebody.

ƒ A velvet hand, a hawk's eye- these we should all have.

ƒ We seldom take great pictures. You have to milk the cow a lot and get lots of milk to make a little piece of cheese.

ƒ You just have to live and life will give you pictures.

ƒ The world is going to pieces and people like Adams and Weston are photographing rocks.

ƒ The picture is good or not from the moment it was caught in the camera.

ƒ Shooting with a Leica is like a long tender kiss, like firing an automatic pistol, like an hour on the analyist's couch.

Henri David Thoreau

ƒ It's not what you look at that matters, it's what you see.

Henri Matisse

ƒ I've been forty years discovering that the queen of all colors is black.

Henrik A. Lundh

ƒ If a photograph stirs the emotions in at least one person, that makes it art. This includes the person who clicked the shutter.

Henry Peach Robinson

ƒ Photograph people as they really are - do not dress them up.

Henry Thoreau

ƒ What I see is mine.

ƒ The question is not what you look at, but what you see.

ƒ Could a greater miracle take place than for us to look through each other's eyes for an instant?

Henry Wessel

ƒ I don't go out looking for pictures. I go out, and if something catches my eye, that's reason enough to photograph it.

Herbert Keppler

f Why doesn't some enterprising camera company go and put together a group of advisers from leading magazines, from successful freelance photographers, from the scientific and industrial and commercial community? Meanwhile, my kingdom for an SLR I can operate when I'm wearing my winter mittens.

f Sitting over a hot computer ain't my idea of fun. My creativity goes almost completely into picture taking. (But) I suppose if I ever retired, I would enjoy learning the Photoshop craft far more than playing golf.

Howard Sochurek

f When I finish a story, I usually feel I am just about qualified to begin it because I have learned so much.

Ignacio Aronovich

ƒ Every time I see a crowd of photographers surrounding a subject my impulse is to go in the opposite direction.

Imogen Cunningham

ƒ I don't think there's any such thing as teaching people photography, other than influencing them a little. People have to be their own learners. They have to have a certain talent.

ƒ Which of my photographs is my favorite? The one I'm going to take tomorrow.

ƒ The thing that's fascinating about portraiture is that nobody is alike.

ƒ Ansel Adams once said to somebody that I was versatile, but what he really meant was that I jump around. I'm never satisfied staying in one spot very long, I couldn't stay with the mountains and I couldn't stay with the trees and I couldn't stay with the rivers. But I can always stay with people, because they really are different.

ƒ There are too many people studying photography now who are never going to make it. You can't give them a formula for making it. You have to have it in you first, you don't learn it. The seeing eye is the important thing.

f Once a woman who does street work said to me, „I've never photographed anyone I haven't asked first". I said to her, „Suppose Cartier-Bresson asked the man who jumped the puddle to do it again - it never would have been the same. Start stealing!".

Irving Penn

f A good photograph is one that communicates a fact, touches the heart and leaves the viewer a changed person for having seen it. It is, in a word, effective.

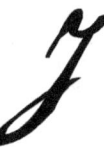

Jacques-Henri Lartigue

ƒ I take photographs with love, so I try to make them art objects. But I make them for myself first and foremost – that is important. If they are art objects at the same time, that's fine with me.

ƒ Photography is something you learn to love very quickly. I know that many, many things are going to ask me to have their pictures taken and I will take them all.

ƒ I have never taken a picture for any other reason than that at that moment it made me happy to do so.

ƒ It's marvellous, marvellous! Nothing will ever be as much fun. I'm going to photograph everything, everything!

ƒ Photography to me is catching a moment which is passing, and which is true.

ƒ
1. Never, never be lazy.
2. Know how to eat well; the right foods in small quantities.
3. Know how to sleep well; the sleep that comes after a good day's work.
4. Know how to appreciate, really appreciate, any good art.

113

5. Know how to enjoy silence, as well as good music.
6. Open your ears to the ideas and suggestions of God.
7. Love God.

Jakub Byrczek

ƒ   Photography is the proof of imperfection of words.

James Elliott

ƒ   When people say photography is not art what they actually mean is their photography is not art.

ƒ   Photography is as easy as you are to please.

James Laropui Keivom

ƒ   It's weird that photographers spend years or even a whole lifetime, trying to capture moments that added together, don't even amount to a couple of hours. I think based on 100.000 shots*(1/125s)=800s=13.3min.

James Nachtwey

ƒ   I used to call myself a war photographer. Now I consider myself as an antiwar photographer.

James Wayner

ƒ   Digital Photography allows us just not to capture memories but it also allows us to create them.

Jan Saudek

ƒ I have no way of portraying the lives of others. I portray my own.

Jarod Kintz

ƒ I want to meet a guy named Art. I'd take him to a museum, hang him on the wall, criticize him, and leave.

Jasna Horvat

ƒ What is actualy art? I grew old, without anyone telling me how to. They call me an artist, even though I don't know nothing about art. My photographs are a hunt for the moment I am caught in myself.

Jay Maisel

ƒ If you are out there shooting, things will happen for you. If you're not out there, you'll only hear about it.

ƒ If the light is great in front of you, you should turn around and see what it is doing behind you.

ƒ Always carry a camera, it's tough to shoot a picture without one.

ƒ I don't care about the quality of the pixels, I care about the quality of the photograph.

Jean Casson

ƒ As far as portraits are concerned I have no doubt that photography is a higher art than painting; it is simpler, more sharp-sighted and more profound.

Jean Cocteau

ƒ A true photographer is as rare as a true poet or a true painter.

Jean Piaget

ƒ What we see changes what we know. What we know changes what we see.

Jean-Luc Godard

ƒ When you photograph a face, you photograph the soul behind it.

Jeff Bridges

ƒ I found that photography was a great way of relaxing on the set.

Jerome Liebling

ƒ My sympathies have always been with the everyday people, the center of my photography.

Jerry Rosen

ƒ Specializing is fine, but wanting to be involved in several aspects of photography has just as much validity.

Jerry Uelsman

f Ultimately, my hope is to amaze myself. The anticipation of discovering new possibilities becomes my greatest joy.

f My creative process begins when I get out with the camera and interact with the world. A camera is truly a license to explore. There are no uninteresting things. There are just uninterested people.

f It's equally hard and labor intensive to create an image on the computer as it is in a darkroom. Believe me.

Jill Freedman

f I hate cheap pictures. I hate pictures that make people look like they're not worth much, just to prove a photographer's point. I hate when they take a picture of someone pickin' their nose or yawning. It's so cheap. A lot of it is a big ego trip. You use people as props instead of as people.

Jim Coe

f I often find photos in the most ordinary places. Many of the subjects are nothing special either. They are just the beautiful things all around us that we don't make the effort to see truly.

f I believe that a spectacular photo of something ordinary is more interesting than an ordinary photo of something spectacular. The latter is about something else, the former is something else.

117

f Potentially wonderful photographs are all around you! The difficulty is in seeing them.

Jim Goldberg

f I have the great privilege of being both witness and storyteller. Intimacy, trust and intuition guide my work.

Jim Richardson

f If you want to be a better photographer, stand in front of more interesting stuff.

Jim Rohn

f You are the average of the five people you spend the most time with.

Jo Spence

f Jo Spence, Photographer: Available for divorces, funerals, illness, social injustice, scenes of domestic violence, exploration of sexuality and any joyful events.

Joan Miró

f You can look at a picture for a week and never think of it again. You can also look at a picture for a second and think of it all your life.

Joe DiMaggio

ƒ The absolute worst thing a person can say about your pictures is, „That's nice". It's the kiss of death.

Joe McNally

ƒ No matter how much crap you gotta plow through to stay alive as a photographer, no matter how many bad assignments, bad days, bad clients, snotty subjects, obnoxious handlers, wigged-out art directors, technical disasters, failures of the mind, body, and will, all the shouldas, couldas, and wouldas that befuddle our brains and creep into our dreams, always remember to make room to shoot what you love. It's the only way to keep your heart beating as a photographer.

ƒ John Loengard, the picture editor at Life, always used to tell me, "If you want something to look interesting, don't light all of it."

ƒ When I was in school, I wanted to be W. Eugene Smith. He was a legendary staffer at Life, a consummate photojournalist, and an architect of the photo essay. He was also kinda crazy.
That was obvious when he came to lecture at Syracuse University and put a glass of milk and a glass of vodka on the lectern. Both were gone at the end of the talk. He was taking questions and I was in the front row, hanging on every word.
Mr. Smith, is the only good light available light?" came the question.
He leaned into the microphone. "Yes," he baritoned, and paused.
A shudder ran through all of us. That was it! No more flash! God's light or nothing!

But then he leaned back into the mic, "By that, I mean, any damn light that's available."
Point taken.

ƒ Don't pack up your camera until you've left the location.

ƒ Unpredictability. Accidents. Not good when you're engaging in, say, brain surgery, but when lighting... wonderful!

ƒ A career in photography is a journey without a destination.

ƒ I can't tell you how many pictures I've missed just 'cause I've been so hell bent on getting the shot I think I want.

ƒ Fill light is the light that you are only aware of when you shut it off.

ƒ Our pictures are our footprints. It's the best way to tell people we were here.

ƒ When shooting a story about someone, their hands should always be on your list to shoot.

Joel Strasser

ƒ A good photographer must love life more than he does photography.

Johann Wolfgang Von Goethe

ƒ The most difficult thing is what is thought to be the simplest; to really see the things which are before your eyes.

John E. Burkowski

ƒ Photographs are like wine, they get better with age.

ƒ Photography. The best cure for a bad memory.

John Cage

ƒ All great art is a form of complaint.

John Loengard

ƒ There are two kinds of photographs: mine and other people's. I never think of what I might do myself when I look at someone else's pictures. There is no subject in the world I have ever wanted to photograph. It's the picture, not he object, that is important to me.

ƒ The reader sees before he ever reads, and may never read if there is nothing to see.

ƒ Photographs don't lie, people lie about photographs.

ƒ Teachers don't work in the summer, and photographers don't shoot in in the middle of the day.

ƒ If I'm very close in on the face, expression doesn't exist. The face becomes a landscape of the lakes of the eyes and the hills of the nose.

John Running

f   A camera gives you a reason to stare.

John Sexton

f   I find the single most valuable tool in the darkroom is my trash can.

f   Pictures you have taken have an influence on those that you are going to make. That's life!

John Steinbeck

f   I hate cameras. They are so much more sure than I am about everything.

John Szarkowski

f   A skillful photographer can photograph anything well.

f   A camera has interesting ideas of its own.

f   Luck is the attentive photographer's best teacher.

John W. Tukey

f   The greatest value of a picture is when it forces us to notice what we never expected to see.

John R. Whiting

f   Advice to photographers: learn technique, then forget it.

John Wooden

f Be quick but don't hurry.

Josef Koudelka

f I have to shoot three cassettes of film a day, even when not „photographing", in order to keep the eye in practice.

Joseph Holmes

f Too many photos make a statement, not enough ask a question.

Julian Flynn

f I find photos of beautiful people boring.

Julian Schnabel

f Traditionally, photography is supposed to capture an event that has passed; but that is not what I'm looking for. Photography brings the past into the present when you look at it.

Julien Smith

f Your content is your agent.

f How to live an uncensored life? Surround yourself by people that offend you and disagree with you and are different then you are. A friend of mine is a pretty well known painter, but his paintings are just ugly, the ugliest things. I almost dilberatly surround myself with these ugly things so I get the impression there is actualy a world somewhere where this is a good thing. And you try to understand that.

Justin Au Eong

f The finished photograph is an extension of the photographer's mind, a window to the heart, soul and values within him.

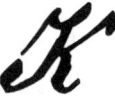

Kai Man Wong

f You can't just look at what's going on, you have to realy see it.

f Don't just shoot, think.

f L lenses won't necessarily give you more bokeh. The main purpose is to lower your bank balance.

Kamilo Nollas

f If you want to do the right thing, you ask for permission first. If not, you shoot the picture and ask for permission later. Sometimes you just shoot and run, it's all part of the game.

Karl Lagerfeld

f What I like about photographs is that they capture a moment that's gone forever, impossible to reproduce.

Keith Carter

f I think the equipment you use has a real, visible influence on the caracter of your photography. You're going to work differently, and make different kinds of pictures, if you have to set up a view camera on a tripod than if you're Lee Friedlander with handheld 35 mm rangefinder. But fundamentally, vision is not about which camera or how many megapixels you have, it's about what you find important. It's all about ideas.

ƒ Sharpness is overrated.

Ken Duncan

ƒ Often the biggest thing blocking the light is your own shadow.

Ken Oosterbroek

ƒ Let the pictures do the talking!

Ken Rockwell

ƒ The camera's only job is to get out of the way of making photographs.

ƒ People who earn less than half of their income from photography are amateurs. This has nothing to do with the quality of their photography.

ƒ No matter how advanced your camera you still need to be responsible for getting it to the right place at the right time and pointing it in the right direction to get the photo you want.

ƒ Photography is the power of observation, not the application of technology.

Keneth Kobre

f Only twelve percent of the people who pick up a news-paper read a story on the front page if no picture accompanies the story.

Kevin Russo

f In order to be a successful photographer, you must possess both vision and focus, neither of which have anything to do with your eyes.

Konrad Dwojak

f A true portrait photographer loves all people because he wants to capture the beauty in every one of them.

Kowtham Kumar K

f A photograph is a click away. A good photograph is a thousands clicks away and a better one, a million clicks away.

Lakshman Iyer

f 1st complaint of family members of a professional photographer – There is no family album.

f It always happens when you're not holding a camera.

f One day photography become photoshopy originality may disappear.

Larry Burrows

f I am very happy with the equipment I have. All I need is time and patience to use it to the fullest degree, plus God on my side to help with the lighting problems – to move the sun, the moon and the stars to the positions of my choice.

Larry Fink

f To photograph a nude without desiring her is the ultimate in perversity.

Larry Wilder

f Keep your finger on the shutter and your feet off the couch.

Laurence Peter

f Competence, like truth, beauty and contact lenses, is in the eye of the beholder.

Lawrence Sackmann

f Your tripod and your camera must be well-fixed but your eyes and mind should be free.

Lawrence Schiller

f Marilyn was a brilliant woman whose public image was based on still photography. I've never photographed anybody who understood so well what the camera would do.

Leonardo da Vinci

f Art is never finished, only abandoned.

Lewis Carroll

f It is my one recreation and I think it should be done well.

Lewis Wickes Hine

f Photography can light-up darkness and expose ignorance

Lieve Blanckaert

f My native language is Dutch, my second is photography.

Lilo Raymond

ƒ It never occurred to me that some day somebody would honor me. What have I done? Fifty good pictures, period!

Linda McCartney

ƒ If you see something that moves you, and then snap it, you keep a moment.

Lisette Model

ƒ The camera is an instrument of detection. We photograph not only what we know, but also what we don't know.

Lord Patrick Lichfield

ƒ Remember that the person you are photographing is 50% of the portrait and you are the other 50%. You need the model as much as he or she needs you. If they don't want to help you, it will be a very dull picture.

Lorne McClinton

ƒ A great shot but pure luck. F8 and being there and being ready.

Luc Delahaye

ƒ I have constraints that are much stronger than any journalist ethics. For me, morals and style are one.

Lucian Perkins

ƒ I hope that, by looking at my photographs, people will develop a better understanding of the world around them and more empathy with the people in it.

Louis Pasteur

ƒ Where observation is concerned, chance favors only the prepared mind.

Mahatma Gandhi

ƒ I believe in equality for everyone, except reporters and photographers.

Malcolm Flowers

ƒ Every time I lift my camera to my eye. I realized that every photo I take is a piece of my life I will never get back, but I will always be able to see again and again.

Man Ray

ƒ What type of camera do you prefer to work with? „None! I have to modify them all. My cameras are all of my own design. I take lenses apart and put them together again and put them on cameras that were not meant for them".

ƒ I photograph what I do not wish to paint, and I paint what I do not wish to photograph.

ƒ In the same spirit, when the automobile arrived, there were those that declared the horse to be the most perfect form of locomotion.

ƒ It has never been my object to record my dreams, just the determination to realize them.

Manuel Alvarez Bravo

f A photographer's main instrument is his eyes. Strange as it may seem, many photographers choose to use the eyes of another photographer, past or present, instead of their own. Those photographers are blind.

Marcel Duchamp

f Unless a picture shocks, it is nothing.

Marcey Jacobson

f I was making photographs of the world long before I was a photographer.

Margaret Bourke-White

f The camera is a remarkable instrument. Saturate yourself with your subject, and the camera will all but take you by the hand and point the way.

f If you want to photograph a man spinning, give some thought to why he spins. Understanding for a photographer is as important as the equipment he uses.

Marie Antoinette

f There is nothing new except what has been forgotten.

Mario Mazziol

f At the end of the day, the photographer must also be a thief, inevitably

Mark Cariaga

ƒ A photographer never tries hard to achieve his desires, a photographer does not need to show off his art because it will speak for it self, a photographer express art through his camera and not by his mouth, a photographer is humble and not self centered, a photographer never puts a value on his art because it is priceless. A photographer brings your imagination to reality.

Mark Twain

ƒ You can't depend on your eyes if your imagination is out of focus.

Mark Wallace

ƒ Black and white is usualy something you use to show form and shape. If you want to show something as a two dimensional object in a realy nice way then black and white should be used for that. Or, if you want to remove some emotion from a photo then black and white is a choice for that.

ƒ To be a good photographer you need to study art in all forms. Not just painting, but sculpture, writing, film making, architecture, typography. It all relates.

ƒ I shoot tons of snapshots, just like anybody else.

ƒ A huge barrier to a lot of photographers is they go in the photoshoot and think „I have to get a great picture".

ƒ I'm gonna try it and I'm gonna fail and I'm gonna fail on purpose.

ƒ If you wanna know how to shoot a wedding, then do a fake wedding.

ƒ Everything is inspiration.

ƒ The world is a classroom.

ƒ It doesn't matter what discipline you're in – if it is a cook, a logger, photographer, an artist, a writer – you can't do no shortcuts.

ƒ Robert Capa's famous quote is usually interpreted as the distance from camera to subject. I also think you can interpret his statement as emotional distance. I believe in putting myself close to my subject physically, and in some instances emotionally as well.

ƒ I also discovered that my photos were much richer when taken after I'd spent time getting to know my subject, even if for a few moments.

ƒ Take some time to forget about aperture values, shutter speeds, lens specifications, and techno babble. Your equipment is simply a tool that will allow you to capture something. The subject is what matters, not the tool you use.

Marsha Cairo

ƒ I like to watch the person viewing my photographs to see if their eyes twinkle or cloud with tears. Does the smile sneak out when they were not exspecting it to.

Then I know I have captured emotion that can be shared.

Martin Parr

ƒ I looked around at what my colleagues were doing, and asked myself, „What relationship has it with what's going on?" I found there was a great distortion of contemporary life. Photographers were interested only in certain things. A visually interesting place, people who were either very rich or very poor, and nostalgia.

ƒ All photography is propaganda.

Mary Ellen Mark

ƒ I just think it's important to be direct and honest with people about why you're photographing them and what you're doing. After all, you are taking some of their soul.

ƒ There is only one reason I've stayed a photographer for so many years. Photography is always challenging.

ƒ Finding the right subject is the hardest part.

ƒ It's not when you press the shutter, but why you press the shutter.

Mason Resnick

ƒ Constantly ask yourself, „what the heck would what I'm looking at look like framed, still, two-dimensional, in black and white?" If the search for an answer gets your heart pumping, makes your throat dry and you become kind of gooey inside, it's love. Don't fight it. Take out that Leica M that you're still paying off and start shooting.

ƒ Shoot a lot of pictures. Experiment. Don't go out with preconceptions of what a picture will look like. That will block you from being receptive to something new and exciting.

Massimo Conti

ƒ Why black and white? Because, you know, black and white is like our life! Sometimes beautiful, sometimes awful. It's a sort of ying and yang and just like our life in the middle you can find a large scale of greys.

Matei Glass

ƒ My favorite photographs speak eloquently, both about and to us.

Matt Hardy

ƒ Beauty can be seen in all things, seeing and composing the beauty is what separates the snapshot from the photograph.

Matt Hevezi

ƒ We eat good food to keep our bodies healthy. I digest good photos as my visual nutrition. If I go too long without looking at good work, I feel starved.

Matthew Jordan Smith

ƒ You build your business shooting for your clients, but you build your career shooting for yourself.

Mattias Klum

ƒ Art is a tool that isn't used enough to effect change.

Max Ernst

ƒ Art has nothing to do with taste. Art is not there to be tasted.

Miguel Syjuco

ƒ Sometimes one waits too long for the perfect moment before snapping the picture. You never realize that all you needed was to change perspective.

Micha Bar-Am

ƒ Working at the scene of the action, I have adopted Robert Capa's saying: „If your photographs aren't good enough, you're not close enough.“ But in retrospect I add a corollary: if you're too close to events, you lose perspective.

Michel Eugène Chevreul

ƒ I was an enemy of photography until my ninety-seventh year, but three years ago I capitulated. *(on his hundredth birthday in 31 August, 1886; during first-ever recorded photographic interview)*

Michael Melford

ƒ   Sometimes it's better to be lucky then good.

Michael Wilson

ƒ   Art is basically what a bunch of collectors and curators say it is, there is no getting around that.

Mike Cindric

ƒ   I can teach technique, but I can't teach vision.

Mike Morse

ƒ   Technical ability aside, the difference is commitment. Some people look at whatever they do as a job and then they want to be good craftsmen. Then there are people who do it as a passion. They really care about it, and it shows in their photographs.

Milan Kundera

ƒ   Memory does not make films, it makes photographs.

Minor White

ƒ   Often while traveling with a camera we arrive just as the sun slips over the horizon of a moment, too late to expose film, only time enough to expose our hearts.

ƒ   I am always mentally photographing everything as practice.

Moose Peterson

f I've been shooting for 30 years. If nothing else you can call it muscle memory. I only shoot when I like what I see in the viewfinder.

Morley Baer

f The best people make the best photographs. *(as oposed to „ best gear makes the best photographs" op.a.)*

Moses Oliver

f Art of photography is a beautiful poem which capture and deliver the pain and feelings of a photographer.

f The photographer is one who use his/her eye as first camera and take the camera to use, secondly.

Muriel Barbery

f Talent consists not in inventing shapes but in causing those that were invisible to emerge.

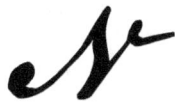

Nan Goldin

ƒ I used to think that I could never lose anyone if I photographed them enough. In fact, my pictures show me how much I've lost.

ƒ I knew from a very early age, that what I saw on TV had nothing to do with real life. So I wanted to make a record of real life. That included having a camera with me at all times.

ƒ There are too many photographers. Try to get involved with something that really matters. And unless you need art to survive, then don't do it.

Naomi Campbell

ƒ I trust pictures, but no pictures made in my world - because I know what goes on.

Nathan Knobler

ƒ The artist photographer knows that there is a great difference between seeing a scene and producing a photographic equivalent.

Neil Leifer

ƒ You have to be ready for luck.

f   I've done four or five pictures that people will remember.

f   Sometimes the simplest picture are the hardest to get.

Nick Nolte

f   Wait a minute - I'm a journalist... I don't take sides, I take pictures. *(as Russel Price in the movie Under fire)*

Norman Mailer

f   Giving a camera to Diane Arbus is like putting a live grenade in the hands of a child.

Norman Parkinson

f   I like to make people look as good as they'd like to look, and with luck, a shade better.

f   The only thing that gets in the way of a really good photograph, is the camera.

f   A photographer without a magazine behind him is like a farmer without fields.

Norman J. Piluke

f   A reality exists in the ability to see it.

f   It is not only the tool that makes a good photograph. It is the person behind it.

O. Winston Link

ƒ The locomotives are black. The coal is black. The tracks are black. The night is black. So what am I going to do with color?

Oliviero Toscani

ƒ Some people look at a picture for thirty seconds, some for years. It doesn't really matter because a picture is like life. You take out of life as much as you are able to take out of life, just as you take out of a picture as much as you can take out of a picture.

Pablo Picasso

f   I have discovered photography. Now I can kill myself. I have nothing else to learn.

f   Now at least we know everything that painting isn't.

f   There are painters who transform the sun into a yellow spot, but there are others who, thank to their art and their intelligence transform the yellow spot into the sun.

f   Two of the most frustrated trades are dentists and photographers- dentists because they want to be doctors, and photographers because they want to be painters.

f   Good artists copy, great artists steal.

f   Everything you can imagine is real.

f   Art is the lie that enables us to realize the truth.

f   The chief enemy of creativity is good sense.

f   There is no abstract art. You must always start with something. Afterward you can remove all traces of reality.

Paul Carvel

f Passion is a positive obsession. Obsession is a negative passion.

Paul Caponigro

f It's one thing to make a picture of what a person looks like, it's another thing to make a portrait of who they are.

f The key is to not let the camera, which depicts nature in so much detail, reveal just what the eye picks up, but what the heart picks up as well.

Paul Delaroche

f From today painting is dead! *(on first seeing a daguerreotype in 1839)*

Paul Gauguin

f I shut my eyes in order to see.

Paul Hill

f Photography should be considered as a language which means that it's grammar and its syntax have to be learnt before the medium can be fully exploited by the photographer.

Paul Lowe

f I took a picture in Grozny of bloodstained footprints in the snow, and that for me has a lot more power than a dead body, because it makes you think much more.

Paul Martin Lester

f The photographic process is so simple. A gorilla took a picture used on a National Geographic cover. There is a danger in that photography is so easy. The taking is easy. The feeling is difficult.

Paul Outerbridge

f One very important difference between color and monochromatic photography is this: in black and white you suggest; in color you state. Much can be implied by suggestion, but statement demands certainty, absolute certainty.

Paul Scriven

f Work for free or for full price, but never for cheap.

Paul Strand

f It is one thing to photograph people. It is another to make others care about them by revealing the core of their humanness.

f Whether a watercolor is inferior to an oil painting, or whether a drawing, an etching, or a photograph is not as important as either, is inconsequent. To have to despise something in order to respect something else is a sign of impotence.

Petar Kürschner

f Photography is the air I breath, the water I drink, the fire I step through, the rock I'm standing on.

146

f I share my feelings through my shots... sometimes there is something I wish to say, but there are no words for it, so here I have my camera, the story teller, and me the director.

Pete Bridgewood

f Landscape photographers are crepuscular creatures, we tend to function most creatively at twilight, be it dawn or dusk.

f I see the photographic image as a three-way relationship between the subject, the viewer and the photographer.

Pete Turner

f „What have I done wrong?" - he said later. „Nothing, I think. I am steadily surprised that there are so many photographers that reject manipulating reality, as if that was wrong. Change reality! If you don't find it, invent it!"

Peter Adams

f Photography is not about cameras, gadgets and gismos. Photography is about photographers. A camera didn't make a great picture any more than a typewriter wrote a great novel.

f Great photography is about depth of feeling, not depth of field.

Peter Kervarec

f Copycats and plagiarists are way worse than thieves! A thief would never put his stolen goods on public display and claim them as his own!

Peter Mendes

f Bad photography, like bad art, is not the fault of the medium, but of the person using the medium.

Percy W. Harris

f Skill in photography is acquired by practice and not by purchase.

Peter Lacey

f No other subject is so indicative of the photographer's taste and talent as the nude.

Peter Stackpole

f I never photographed a subject more than one or two exposures. Then I'd go on to something else. I don't admire photographers who use motors.

Philip Wayner

f The camera is a time machine and you are the pilot. It captures the present so that someone in the future can see a moment recorded in the past as seen by you.

Philippe Halsman

f   I drifted into photography like one drifts into prostitution. First I did it to please myself, then I did it to please my friends, and eventually I did it for the money.

f   I am often asked which picture is my favorite. This is like asking a mother which child she likes the most.

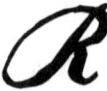

Raghu Rai

ƒ A photograph has picked up a fact of life, and that fact will live forever.

Ralph Auletta

ƒ After 40 years of ingesting every aspect of photographic science and composition, I still find the camera to be an endlessly intriguing partner that challenges my imagination and knowledge. All that with only 3 variables of shutter speed, aperture and focal length.

Ralph Bartolomew Jr.

ƒ While some people are afraid of of snakes, others have phobias about high places - I'm scared of long exposures.

Ralph Gibson

ƒ Even though fixed in time, a photograph evokes as much feeling as that which comes from music or dance. Whatever the mode – from the snapshot to the decisive moment to multi-media montage – the intent and purpose of photography is to render in visual terms feelings and experiences that often elude the ability of words to describe. In any case, the eyes have it, and the imagination will always soar farther than was expected.

Ralph Waldo Emerson

ƒ Art is not to be found by touring to Egypt, China, or Peru; if you cannot find it at your own door, you will never find it.

ƒ Do not call yourself an „artist-photographer" and make „artist-painters" and „artist-sculptors" laugh; call yourself a photographer and wait for artists to call you brother.

Raymond Depardon

ƒ I don't regret the numerous pictures of Brigitte Bardot, but I'd rather have a good photograph of my father.

Ren Garcia

ƒ Trying to live up to yourself is the most trying thing.

Rene Magritte

ƒ Everything that is visible hides something that is invisible.

Rich Remsberg

ƒ Photography is not a contest... It's about being a witness to your times.

Richard Avedon

ƒ My portraits are more about me than they are about the people I photograph.

ƒ All photographs are accurate. None of them is the truth.

ƒ I've worked out of a series of no's. No to exquisite light, no to apparent compositions, no to the seduction of poses or narrative. And all these no's force me to the „yes". I have a white background. I have the person I'm interested in and the thing that happens between us.

Richard Pollard

ƒ There's a hell of a difference between a very good photographer and an extraordinary one. The great ones have a passion about their pictures... That's all they care about.

Richard Stafford

ƒ Behold the Photographer! He hath been smitten by the Shutter Beetle, He Feareth the Light, and spendeth Many Wearisome Hours in the Room Called Dark. He soweth not, neither does he reap, but Seeketh Ever the Grain that is Fine. It has been Thus since the Beginning, even unto One Thousand One, One Thousand Two, One Thousand Three. Ask of the Populace - is he a man who Posesseth All his senses? Lo! The answer is in the Negative.

Rick Sammon

f   The camera looks both ways.

Rineke Dijkstra

f   I don't need to know anything about the people I photograph, but it's important that I recognize something about myself in them.

Robert Adams

f   No place is boring, if you've had a good night's sleep and have a pocket full of unexposed film.

f   Timothy O'Sullivan was, it seems to me, the greatest of the photographers because he understood nature first as architecture.

Robert Andrejaš

f   In the flood of personal exhibitions of photography of various „artists", one should know that even the hanging of the clothes is an exhibition, of no less artistic value then the most of those exhibitions.

f   The result you get by using program automatic on cameras only proves that Murphy was right when he said that „What the fool knows, only a fool does".

Robert Brault

f   It pleases me to take amateur photographs of my garden, and it pleases my garden to make my photographs look professional.

153

Robert Bresson

𝑓 When you do not know what you are doing and what you are doing is the best - that is inspiration.

𝑓 Make visible what, without you, might perhaps never have been seen.

Robert Capa

𝑓 If your photos aren't good enough, then you're not close enough.

𝑓 Q: Do you really distance yourself from your subject? I mean, what would you do if you were presented with a young girl burning to death?
A: About 1/60 at f5.6.

𝑓 The pictures are there, and you just take them

𝑓 This war is like an actress who is getting old. It is less and less photogenic and more and more dangerous.

𝑓 Like the people you shoot and let them know it.

Robert Doisneau

𝑓 If I knew how to take a good photograph, I'd do it every time.

Robert Farber

𝑓 If you want to make good photographs, a camera has to be second nature to you. Devoting too much attention to technical decisions can interfere with your creative processes.

Robert Frank

f When people look at my pictures I want them to feel the way they do when they want to read a line of a poem twice.

f Black and white are the colors of photography. To me, they symbolize the alternatives of hope and despair to which mankind is subjected.

f My photographs are not planned or composed in advance, and I do not anticipate that the onlooker will share my viewpoint. However, I feel that if my photograph leaves an image on his mind, something has been accomplished.

f I've never been successful at making films, really. I've never been able to do it right. And there's something terrific about that. There's something good about being a failure--it keeps you going.

Robert Mapplethorpe

f I went into photography because it seemed like the perfect vehicle for commenting on the madness of today's existence.

f I'm looking for the unexpected. I'm looking for things I've never seen before.

Roberto Calasso

f Such is the power of the image: It heals only those who know what it is. For everybody else, it is an illness.

Rochelle Car

ƒ Art has a voice - let it speak.

Roland Barthes

ƒ Usually the amateur is defined as an immature state of the artist: someone who cannot — or will not — achieve the mastery of a profession. But in the field of photographic practice, it is the amateur, on the contrary, who is the assumption of the professional: for it is he who stands closer to the noeme of photography.

Rolando Gomez

ƒ Light is to an image as blood is to the body.

Ronald Reagan

ƒ I like photographers — you don't ask questions.

ƒ Just remember my best side is my right side — my far right side.

Rosie O'Donnell

ƒ I know the best moments can never be captured on film, even as I spend nearly half my life trying to do just that.

Roy DeCarava

ƒ You should be able to look at me and see my work. You should be able to look at my work and see me.

Rumio Sato

f I don't take pictures for the sake of photographing. I take photographs to express what's going on inside of me. Photography turned out to be the most handy tool.

Ryan Holiday

f You don't have to believe in the rules, you don't have to agree with the rules, but you have to abide by the rules.

Salman Rushdie

ƒ A photograph is a moral decision taken in one eighth of a second.

Salvador Dali

ƒ Surrealism is destructive, but it destroys only what it considers to be shackles limiting our vision.

Sam Abell

ƒ I see something special and show it to the camera. The moment is held until someone sees it. Then it is theirs.

ƒ Actually, ambition won't get you that far. You'll shift gears. You'll see something that's shinier. But if you believe... then you're the long-distance runner.

ƒ My best work is often almost unconscious and occurs ahead of my ability to understand it.

ƒ It matters little how much equipment we use; it matters much that we be masters of all we do use.

Sam Haskings

ƒ Artists don't owe the world anything, least of all explanations.

Sarah Leen

f I like difficult places. I like untrod territory - places other people haven't done. I need to be out of my elements so my vision isn't contaminated by what others have done. Those places are difficult in creature comforts, but there's a freshness to them.

Scott Adams

f Creativity is allowing yourself to make mistakes. Art is knowing which ones to keep.

Scott Fleming

f I thought I made a mistake once but it turned out it was a creative moment.

Sebastiao Salgado

f It's not the photographer who makes the picture, but the person being photographed.

Sergio Larrain

f A good picture is born from a state of grace. Grace becomes manifest when one is freed from conventions, free as a child in his first discovery of reality. The game is then to organize the triangle.

Seth Godin

f Art is what we call the thing an artist does. It's not the medium or the oil or the price or whether it hangs on a wall or you eat it. What matters, what makes it art, is that the person who made it overcame the resistance, ignored the voice of doubt and made something worth making. Something risky. Something human. Art is not in the eye of the beholder. It's in the soul of the artist.

Sharon Wax

f When the shutter closes the world opens!

Sid Grossman

f The function of the photographer is to help people understand the world around them.

Sir Joshua Reynolds

f A room hung with pictures is a room hung with thoughts.

Stanko Abadžić

f Mass media bombard us with images of blood and tears. It's high time we showed interest in beauty and aesthetics, not lust in wars and catastrophes.

Stefan Lorant

f The camera should be like the notebook of a trained reporter, to record events as they happen, without trying to stop them to make a picture.

Stephen Johnson

f Delay pushing the shutter until you decide what you are photographing.

Steve Coleman

ƒ If you stop photographing things, and start to photograph light, you will amaze yourself.

ƒ I only use one light... the sun.

ƒ Many photographers photograph the world the way it is. I photograph the world the way I would like the world to be.

ƒ Change your perspective.

ƒ If you see something beautiful, take a picture of it. The world needs to see more beauty.

ƒ Take your camera off automatic. You are the photographer.

ƒ Beware of the camera with all the smart technology... It can ruin you as a photographer.

ƒ A camera exposes more than just an image. It also exposes the photographer.

Steve Denby

ƒ The world is one huge canvas, find your location and expose your film passionately!

ƒ When people ask what equipment I use I tell them my eyes!

ƒ The camera is just a viewfinder with a recording device, as it can't think!

Steve Silberman

 ƒ Film is cheaper than opportunity

Stu Jenks

 ƒ Selenium is weird stuff. It makes the photograph permanent, but it kills the photographer.

 ƒ What I really enjoy about night shooting is that I'm not just recording fractions of a second of time, but minutes, and sometimes hours of time on film.

 ƒ I used to talk more about my work, back when my work wasn't as good.

Susan Sontag

 ƒ All photographs are memento mori. To take a photograph is to participate in another person's (or thing's) mortality, vulnerability, mutability. Precisely by slicing out this moment and freezing it, all photographs testify to time's relentless melt.

 ƒ Today everything exists to end in a photograph.

 ƒ Time eventually positions most photographs, even the most amateurish, at the level of art.

 ƒ Travel becomes a strategy for accumulating photographs.

Sydney Cabbie

 ƒ Photography is not a bad past-time for people who can't paint.

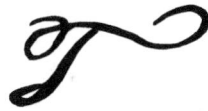

Tallulah Bankhead

ƒ They used to photograph Shirley Temple through gauze. They should photograph me through linoleum.

Ted Grant

ƒ When you photograph people in color, you photograph their clothes. But when you photograph people in Black and white, you photograph their souls!

ƒ

You can have the best work in the world and if you don't put it in front of people, you'll never get anywhere.

Ted Orland

ƒ There's nothing wrong with 35mm, that a 5X4 (Hasselblad) can't put right.

Tedric A. Garrison

ƒ Remember... light is your crayon, and there's always another color in the box.

ƒ A snap shot is a two-dimensional piece of paper. A photograph is a three-dimensional work of art.

Thomas Hoepker

f You are lucky if you take one, maybe two good pictures in a year.

Thomas Robinson

f I am a messenger of the beauty of creation.

Tielhard Chardin

f The more one looks, the more one sees. And the more one sees, the better one knows where to look.

Tiffany Madison

f Women that can work a camera with ease often work men just as effortlessly for both require the same commitment to vanity and manipulation.

Tim Mantoani

f A camera, like a guitar, is just a box with a hole in it. Until it is placed in the hands of a true artist, it will not make a music, only noise.

f Great photographers work on impulse, on their gut. They listen to that voice in the back of their head even when it is telling them to do something that common sense tells them not to.

f Photographers are collectors, every one of them. Some collect bits and pieces of various subjects while others become obsessed with only one. We should be thankful to these compulsive individuals who can not quit. It is through their obsession that history is

164

archived, various stories are collected and told with their single voice running through them, preserved for those that follow.

Timothy Allen

f It can be a trap of the photographer to think that his or her best pictures were the ones that were hardest to get.

Tina Manley

f I prefer to photograph people and try to capture an emotion which can be universally understood. Photography is the language I use to translate other cultures.

Tom Hubbard

f Photojournalists not only march to a different drummer, they have to write the music as they march.

Tom Sperduto

f Photography is my passion. With my photography, I attempt to capture the beauty, frailty, and strength of the human spirit.

f Photography to me is therapeutic. It's a way for me to release and express emotion. A good day taking pictures is equivalent to a good visit to an expensive therapist.

f Sometimes photography can be as much hiding as seeing. There is nothing better than having a camera at a boring party.

Toni Frissel

f Here are faces that I have found memorable. If they are not all as happy as kings, it is because in this imperfect world and these hazardous times, the camera's eye, like the eye of a child, often sees true.

Tony Benn

f Most things in life are moments of pleasure and a lifetime of embarrassment; photography is a moment of embarrassment and a lifetime of pleasure.

Trent Parke

f I am forever chasing light. Light turns the ordinary into the magical.

T. S. Eliot

f The progress of an artist is a continual self-sacrifice, a continual extinction of personality.

Ty Holland

f A photograph is the pause button on life.

Tyra Banks

f There are 3 key things for good photography: the camera, lighting and... photoshop

Vernon Trent

ƒ Amateurs worry about equipment, professionals worry about money, masters worry about light, I just take pictures.

Vicki Goldberg

ƒ When photography was invented it was thought to be an equivalent to truth, it was truth with a capital "T".

Vincent Laforet

ƒ Whenever I use different type of lenses I try not to let the lens tell me what to do.

ƒ If I see a pack of photographers at one place I go the oposite direction every time.

ƒ Welcome change.

ƒ The one thing you learn as a photojournalist is that things tend to happen in patterns.

ƒ A lot of times you have your frame very much in mind and you're waiting for things to fall in place.

ƒ Teaching is one of the best things you can give back to people.

Vincent van Gogh

f There is nothing more truly artistic than to love people.

f Art is to console those who are broken by life.

Vincent Versace

f Photoshop is not a verb. It is a noun. It is the means to an end, not the end itself.

Vittore Buzzi

f I live to take pictures, I take pictures to live.

f Your legs will take you where others dare not. Save the money not for the equipment but for a good pair of shoes.

W. Eugene Smith

f Never have I found the limits of the photographic potential. Every horizon, upon being reached, reveals another beckoning in the distance. Always, I am on the threshold.

f What uses having a great depth of field, if there is not an adequate depth of feeling?

f Available light is any damn light that is available!

Walker Evans

f Stare. It is the way to educate your eye, and more. Stare, pry, listen, eavesdrop. Die knowing something. You are not here long.

f Color tends to corrupt photography and absolute color corrupts absolutely. There are four simple words for the matter which must be whispered: color photography is vulgar. When the point of a picture subject is precisely the vulgarity then only color film can be used validly.

f A few years later after acquiring a Polaroid camera: "Paradox is a habit of mine. Now I am going to devote myself with great care to my work in color."

Walter De Mulder

ƒ I don't press the shutter without beeing sure that the picture isn't good enough to hang in a gallery.

Walter Sickert

ƒ Photography, like alcohol, should only be allowed to those who can do without it.

Wayne Paulo

ƒ We all look but do we see?

ƒ Photography! Acquiring the knowledge and tools to express your artistic vision.

Willard Morgan

ƒ Photography will be the twentieth-century art and the international language.

William Albert Allard

ƒ I think the 50mm lens is an extremely good discipline lens; it requires you to see in a more refined way, not just tighter.

William Henry Fox Talbot

ƒ How charming it would be if it were possible to cause these natural images to imprint themselves durable and remain fixed upon the paper! And why should it not be possible? I asked myself.

William Klein

f Be yourself. I much prefer seeing something, even it is clumsy, that doesn't look like somebody else's work.

William Thackeray

f The two most engaging powers of a photograph are to make new things familiar and familiar things new.

Wladyslaw Pawelec

f Generally, the idea of nude photography is unambiguously identified with the image of female body. Only a naked woman looks naturally. A naked man looks not dressed.

Wynn Bullock

f I didn't want to tell the tree or weed what it was. I wanted it to tell me something and through me express its meaning in nature.

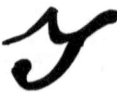

Yann Arthus-Bertrand

f The Earth is art, the photographer is only a witness

Yann Martel

f If we, citizens, do not support our artists, then we sacrifice our imagination on the altar of crude reality and we end up believing in nothing and having worthless dreams.

Yousuf Karsh

f Look and think before opening the shutter. The heart and mind are the true lens of the camera.

f Within every man and woman a secret is hidden, and as a photographer it is my task to reveal it if I can.

Zack Arias

ƒ Never let them see you sweat... Never let them smell you sweat either.

ƒ Shoot for the stars... But not for the porn stars.

Zakir Khan

ƒ For me, photography is a virtue, a charity if done to value the people around.

Anonymous

ƒ I think a photography class should be a requirement in all educational programs because it makes you see the world rather than just look at it.

ƒ Every time someone tells me how sharp my photos are, I assume that it isn't a very interesting photograph. If it were, they would have more to say.

ƒ One photo out of focus is a mistake, ten photo out of focus are an experimentation, one hundred photo out of focus are a style.

ƒ Some of us cynics say that „the quickest way to make a million dollars in photography, is to start with two million dollars".

ƒ Amateurs talk about equipment. Professionals talk about photos.

ƒ Photographers see the world in only fractions of a second.

ƒ f8 and being there. (*Also attributed to Lorne McClinton)*

ƒ I take pictures like Jimmy Page, and I play guitar like Ansel Adams.

ƒ Photography is like a lemon, sour to some, but lemonade to others.

ƒ If you saw a man drowning and you could either save him or photograph the event... what kind of film would you use?

ƒ You didn't compromise on your camera. You shouldn't on your lenses.

ƒ The quickest way to make money at photography is to sell your camera.

ƒ If an old man asks a young girl for a date...
That's his business.
If the young girl accepts...
That's her business.
If the old man and the girl decide to marry...
That's their business.
However, if they want great wedding photographs...
That's my business!

ƒ Success is what happens when 10,000 hours of preparation meet with one moment of opportunity.

ƒ The only 'bad light' is the absence of light altogether.

ƒ Amateurs look for sharpness. Professionals look for sales. Artists look for light.

ƒ Hard work beats talent when talent doesn't work hard. *(Advice given to Stuart Scott)*

ƒ The best camera is the one you left at home. *(Zack Arias' old studio manager; as oposed to Chase Jarvis: The best camera is the one that's with you., op.ed.)*

www.ingramcontent.com/pod-product-compliance
Lightning Source LLC
Chambersburg PA
CBHW051312220526
45468CB00004B/1308